Idea as Model

Introduction by Richard Pommer

Catalogue 3

Published by the Institute for
Architecture and Urban Studies and
Rizzoli International Publications, Inc.

Contents

Editors
Kenneth Frampton
Silvia Kolbowski

Editorial Assistant
Patricia Bates

Designer
Massimo Vignelli

Design Coordinator
Abigail Moseley

Production
Marguerite McGoldrick

Editorial Consultant
Joan Ockman

**IAUS Exhibition Catalogues
Program Co-Directors**
Kenneth Frampton
Silvia Kolbowski

**Idea as Model
Exhibition Director**
Andrew MacNair

**Idea as Model
Exhibition Coordinator**
William Eitner

First published in the United States of America in 1981 by Rizzoli International Publications, Inc. 712 Fifth Avenue, New York, N.Y. 10019

© The Institute for Architecture and Urban Studies
8 West 40th Street
New York, N.Y. 10018

All rights reserved. No part of this book may be reproduced in any manner whatsoever without permission in writing from Rizzoli International Publications, Inc.
Library of Congress Catalogue Card Number 80-54700
ISBN 0-8478-0376-7

Typography by Myrel Chernick
Printed by Morgan Press, Inc.

Cover:
Collage made for a limited edition of posters for the "Idea as Model" exhibition, 1976. Michael Graves. Paper, wood, paint.

Preface

Peter Eisenman

This exhibition had its origins in a long-standing intuition of mine that a model of a building could be something other than a narrative record of a project or a building. It seemed that models, like architectural drawings, could well have an artistic or conceptual existence of their own, one which was relatively independent of the project that they represented.

In 1976, as a result of this initial interest, the Institute decided to mount an exhibition whose prime intent was to test and then demonstrate this hypothesis of the conceptual model. We wanted to show that many architects were already using models in this way by documenting a variety of their approaches. In addition, we hoped that in doing so we might also encourage other architects to adopt the idea of a model as a conceptual as opposed to narrative tool, as part of their design process. We wanted to suggest that the model, like the drawing, could have an almost unconscious, unpremeditated, even generative, effect on the design process, that is, a similar effect to that of a two-dimensional projection to provoke unforseen "structural" developments or even modes of perception in the process of design. So, possibly, a three-dimensional projection could provide a similar kind of conceptual feedback.

The first exhibition tended to reveal rather explicitly those architects who were and were not using models to such ends, and it also indicated the variety of representational modes which being were employed at the time. Given the delayed publication of this catalogue we thought it might be interesting to ask the same participants to submit new models which were made in the four-year period between the initial exhibition and this publication.

The introductory essay and postscript by Richard Pommer are lucid discussions of both the shortcomings and discoveries of the two endeavors. The more general essay by Christian Hubert addresses the theoretical underpinnings of the working of the model as a form of representation.

Installation view of exhibition at the Institute for Architecture and Urban Studies, New York, 1976.

1

Plaster architectonic model, ca. 1926.
Kasimir Malevich. Reconstructed
from twenty-nine original elements
and forty reconstructed elements by
The Centre Georges Pompidou, 1978.

2

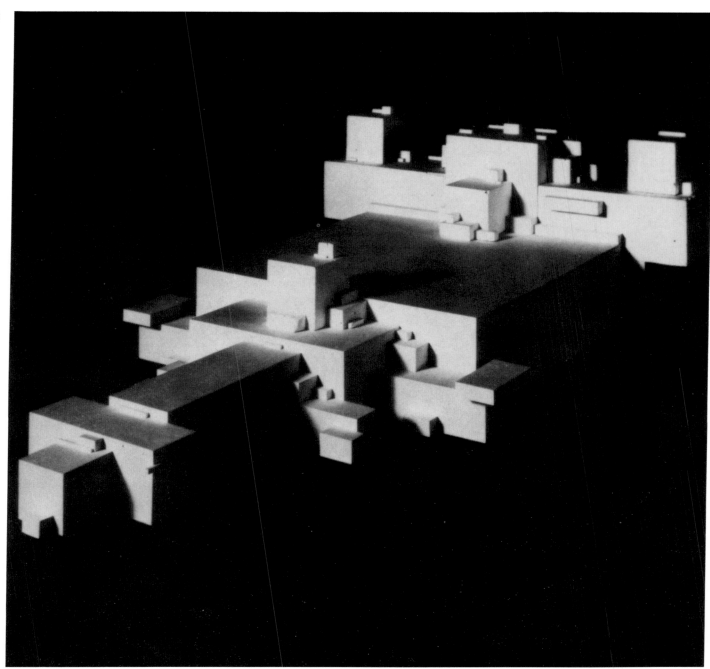

The Idea of "Idea as Model"

Richard Pommer

The purpose of this exhibition is to clarify new means of investigating architecture in three-dimensional form. We do not seek to assemble models of buildings as propaganda for persuading clients, but rather as studies of a hypothesis, a problem, or an idea of architecture.
Excerpt from a letter sent by the Institute to solicit models for the exhibition

An exhibition devoted to ideas of architecture—ideas of its nature and meaning—ought to have been welcome in some circles, and perhaps successful. Some architects have been trying for a decade or more, after all, to escape the deadweight of an architecture too real to be true. Often they seem to have thought of architectural ideas as the opposite of reality, in Platonic conflict with the world, and not merely as applied reason or imagination. Yet it should be added immediately that their ideas have not been utopian or expressionistic or futuristic in the manner of the 1920s or again of the 1960s. These architects have been too little confident of an alternative reality for any of that; their proposals and their buildings recall us to mind or art, not to a vision or hope.

In comparable efforts, artists have stolen much of the ground from architects. Barnett Newman and Tony Smith (fig. 3) have rivaled architecture's scale, Donald Judd its stereometry (fig. 4), Carl Andre its modularity (fig. 2), Sol LeWitt its structures of ideas in space (fig. 7), Robert Smithson (fig. 5) and Michael Heizer (fig. 6) its presence in landscape, and so forth. Robert Morris and others have appropriated its maps, aerial photos, scale drawings, and models for their own (fig. 1). This work would seem to invite some response from architects.

But why not an exhibition of drawings instead of models? Drawings are closer to ideas—sketches to initial conceptions, elevations to proportional schemata, plans to geometric diagrams, views to dreams. Models by contrast usually are dumb, for show and the study of appearances. Perhaps the hope was to present difficult ideas more effectively to the public, but that would have been no more than another form of "propaganda for persuading clients," though in this event unpaying clients.

Models can, however, provide an illusion of reality, without being compromised by it. The value placed on reality and the conceptions of it, not the medium of the representation, are the essential matters. When the building is being built or when its material existence comes to define architecture, as it did especially in the post war decades, then "studies of a hypothesis" are an embarrassment. But when buildings seem unreal, when the Beaux-Arts looks false, or SOM empty, then idea and all of its manifestations in drawing, models, or buildings, will preempt reality. That is to say, in times of radical change.

Perhaps twice in this century architecture has shifted direction sharply enough to call up idea in the form of models: in the twenties, with Mies's glass skyscraper model (fig. 8), Van Doesburg and Van Eesteren's models of the Rosenberg House (fig. 9), Malevich's series of models (frontispiece), and especially Le Corbusier's Citrohan project (fig.11), which remains the paradigm for the elevation of the model to the realm of idea; and again briefly in the early sixties, at the time of the dissolution of the International Style, with Kiesler's Endless House (fig. 10), Kahn's Goldenberg House (fig. 12) or Luanda Consulate (fig. 13), and Venturi's Frug House. At such times even newly built work seems unreal, for example the realizations of the Citrohan at Weissenhof or Antwerp, "cardboard architecture."

Some precedents, then, for the idea of the exhibition, and some parallels. Yet the exhibition did not come off well, and it may be worth asking why. Some architects chose to defy the intent of the invitation, and to exhibit models for built or commissioned works—thus Robert A.M. Stern, Jaquelin Robertson, Charles Gwathmey, Richard Meier. For them the executed work with all of the particularities of its clients and site (the site is shown in the models of Stern, Gwathmey, and Tod Williams) remains the standard by which all else is judged. Even Meier's Pound Ridge House model, though it may be the most poetic formulation of his theme of movement to a private realm, as if to a tree house in a white wood, achieves its meaning solely as a preparation for the building. Robert Stern, by showing a client's model meant for judging a New York townhouse facade against its neighbors, turned the exhibit into a polemical statement

1

4

2

3

4

Observatory, *1977. Robert Morris.*
Model. Hammered lead on wood.

Twelfth Copper Corner, *1975. Carl*
Andre. Copper.

Last, *Cleveland, Ohio, 1979. Tony*
Smith. Painted steel.

4 Untitled, *1967. Donald Judd. Burnt*
sienna enamel on cold rolled steel.
Eight units, 48" x 48" x 48" each at
12" intervals.

5 Spiral Jetty, *1970. Robert Smithson.*

6 Complex One, *1972-1976.*
Michael Heizer.

7 Modular Cube, *1966. Sol Lewitt.*
Painted aluminum, 60" x 60" x 60".

5

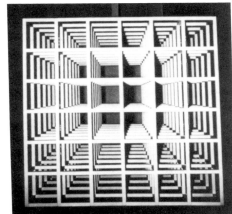

7

6

8 *Project for a glass skyscraper,*
1920-1921. Mies van der Rohe. Model.

9 *Leonce Rosenberg House, 1923. Theo*
van Doesburg and Cor van Eesteren.
Model.

8

9

for this position. Charles Moore exemplified it in a special way, showing a plastic mold in low relief of the plan of a house for a blind client who could read it like a map in Braille. Perhaps only such a seemingly circumstantial event could provide so effective a model of Moore's particularistic architecture with its incitement to exploratory movement.

Others played games with the theme, as required by the residual aesthetic of Pop, or attitudes toward the Institute. Stanley Tigerman toyed with cars and animal cracker boxes; Stuart Wrede wet the floor with a Grass Cube House; William Ellis demonstrated a detached facade by zippering its fly. In an earlier moment we might have had Robert Venturi's Franklin Circle Fountain (fig. 14), Claes Oldenburg's Lipstick (fig. 15), or Hans Hollein's Aircraft Carrier (fig. 16). Another exhibit may have had greater possibilities. The late Gordon Matta-Clark wanted to show photographs of vandalized New York windows against panes broken for the occasion at the Institute, but at the last minute, with the cold air coming in, his exhibit was pulled. A pity, whatever the reasons: it would have called attention to the rival conceptions of younger artists, who often seem less afraid of social statements than these architects do.

A few architects raised questions about the nature of the model as a medium. Rafael Moneo attacked the problem directly, showing a photograph of a building he had constructed in Madrid, together with an axonometric drawing of the building and a model in relief of the axonometric (not of the building). The model was the most tangible representation but the most deceptive one; the drawing was at once the most abstract and the most clearly itself—the beginning of a speculation which few have tried before. Michael Graves hung two models in low relief representing low-relief facades from two recent house projects. It is usually said that Graves's work is the closest of all to painting, but these models illustrate that, as in Frank Stella's recent work, the distinction between painting and sculpture has gone. And since the doors and windows in the models can and perhaps must be read as patches and colors rather than as scale indicators, the distinction between model and buildings begins to blur too. But the models only begin to

10 Endless House, *1959-1961.*
*Frederick Kiesler. Cement over wire
mesh, 39" x 96" x 42".*

11 *Citrohan House, 1921.
Le Corbusier. Model.*

12 *Morton Goldenberg House, Rydal,
Pennsylvania, 1959. Louis Kahn.
Model.*

13 *United States Consulate Buildings,
Luanda, Angola, 1959-1961.
Louis Kahn. Model.*

10

11

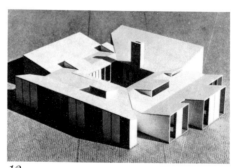

12

13

14 Franklin Circle Fountain
Competition, 1964. Venturi and
Rauch. Model.

15 Lipstick Monument in situ at Yale
University, 1969. Claes Oldenburg.

16 Carriercity in Landscape: Project,
1964. Hans Hollein. Photomontage.

8

14

15

make clear the richness and nuance of Graves's architectural discourse, which is what matters, not "an idea."

Another group of models presented architectural conceits or attitudes toward architecture rather than a rational idea of it. Some looked back to the Mediterranean (once again) for a truer architecture. Jorge Silvetti and Rodolfo Machado compiled a source book of ancient structures; Diana Agrest abstracted the public spine from her private house stepped down a coastal hill; Mario Gandelsonas and Agrest plotted a retrieval of the Neoclassical moment between history and abstraction; Pancho Guedes carved a primitive temple like the models found in ancient Greek sites; Leon Krier and Massimo Scolari placed surrogate pylons of themselves to discourse across a narrow strait. But some labored too hard in joining "Club Med" to succeed in bringing visitors with them.

Raimund Abraham's "House without Rooms," by contrast, exists uncannily: it seems to be more a building than a model. Its plan, section, and elevation (not shown in the exhibition) are drawn as if they too were inhabited. Like a long-standing building, it presses memories upon us; but like models with a magical or religious function, such as primitive temples and house models and reliquaries in the shape of buildings, it represents or anticipates a dwelling or entombment within it. It is also, unlike the other exhibits, a work of sculpture, a rival of the work of artists. It stands on a base, or rather on two bases, and the lower one, the eroded cube, is also the upper part of Abraham's Earth-Cloud House. Abraham's architecture exists in ourselves, to be brought forth equally in drawings, models, buildings, and sculpture, wherever we are called into it. His darkness, which we know in Beckett or Beuys or faintly in Cornell, is the rarest sensibility in modern architecture, though it ought not to be.

John Hejduk, who has been elucidating some metaphors of existence in a long series of projects, brought together four models from his Bye House project and from a later series. Side by side, they suggested other ideas: formally and literally, "the compression of space" from the long entry and cubic volume of the first Bye House project to the

shrunken access and chamber of the latest work—experientially and metaphorically, a quicker and harsher passage to isolation. The ideas would seem to have arisen, as may be true of Hejduk's other work, not from within, but from observation of the drawings and models themselves, from form to metaphor.

The model by Peter Eisenman is central to an evaluation of the exhibition. Alone among the exhibits, it was an attempt to represent an idea of pure reason. Generated by the drawings for his earlier House II, it nevertheless invoked his more current preoccupations with an architecture which might exist without indications of scale, like the sculptures of Donald Judd, but as architecture all the same. Out of these concerns of Eisenman's the exhibition was conceived.

Yet in Eisenman's own estimate at the close of the exhibition, the model failed to meet the conditions of the exhibition because it merely represented an idea fully elaborated already in drawings (and buildings), with the chief purpose of making this idea understandable to the public. A harsh judgment, which confirms equally the grandeur of the intellectual pursuit and its peripheral course today.

For in its recoil from material reality, architectural speculation has not moved to the edges of pure idea. Nothing so radical! It has moved toward allusion; it has evoked the theater and movies, myth and architectural history, landscapes and paintings, and the processes of allusion themselves—reality at a distance. Allusive sensibility might be said to characterize the best work, despite all the obvious differences, of Meier and of Stern, of Graves and of Moore, of Machado and Silvetti, of Krier and Hejduk and Abraham, among others. But such a sensibility is not well conveyed in typical models or architectural drawings, or in any exhibition on demand. It is too dependent on nuance, circumstance, setting, detail, and even, ironically, on real buildings.

Figure Credits
IAUS Exhibition installation view by William Eitner.
Frontispiece reprinted from *Malevitch*, Centre Georges Pompidou, 1980.

3 Courtesy of The Pace Gallery, New York.
4 Photograph by Rudolph Burckhardt. Courtesy of Leo Castelli Gallery, New York.
5 Photograph by Gianfranco Gorgoni. Courtesy of the Estate of Robert Smithson.
6 Photograph by Gianfranco Gorgoni. Courtesy of Xavier Fourcade, Inc., New York.
7 Courtesy of the Museum of Modern Art, New York.
10 Courtesy of Andre Emerich Gallery, New York.
16 Collection, The Museum of Modern Art, New York. Gift of Philip Johnson.

Postscript to a Post-Mortem

Richard Pommer

Four years have passed since the close of the exhibition "Idea as Model." In the interval, architecture has changed in several ways which may explain some of the obscurities of the exhibition and of my essay on it.

First, models and drawings have been taken up by the galleries. Architects have stopped pretending that they are above selling their ideas as works of art; collectors have learned that an architectural drawing may be worth more than an Arbus or even an Atget. At Max Protetch's gallery, Michael Graves, John Hejduk, Aldo Rossi, Massimo Scolari, Charles Moore, and Leon Krier alternate with painters and sculptors; at Leo Castelli's Downtown, house models are sold to the highest bidder just like the new works of Alice Aycock, or Siah Armajani, and Mary Miss (fig. 1) elsewhere around town. Architects have lost their virginity. No longer is it possible to believe that confining architecture to paper and cardboard will keep it free from the dirty ways of the street. Architectural drawings and models have the same commercial currency as a Leroy Neiman or a Robert Arneson. An architectural exhibition called "Idea as Model" would be as pretentious and superfluous today as one called "The Sketch (or Maquette) as Idea." For better and worse, architecture is merely one of the arts.

Second, and more important, the modernists have lost the war; or to be more specific, Peter Eisenman, the last of the modernists, has been outflanked. The exhibition of 1976 was really a response by Eisenman to Arthur Drexler's exhibition of the Ecole des Beaux-Arts at the Museum of Modern Art the year before. Drexler argued in his thoughtful catalogue essay that modern architecture, in its pretense to objectivity, had relied on the material reality of models, whereas the freer, fictive architecture of the Beaux-Arts had depended on the illusions of drawings. Eisenman's exhibition was an attempt to prove the contrary, that models, like his architecture, could represent ideas beyond the objective concerns of conventional modern architecture.

As modernism went down to defeat, drawings once again became the preeminent architectural medium they usually had been in the past. But they did not drive out models. On the contrary, the typical architectural exhibition today—such as that of Rossi, Hejduk, or Graves (his second one) at Max Protetch's—consists of many different kinds of drawings and models for each project or building: thumbnail sketches, plans, occasional sections, detailed elevations, views, collages, fantasies, wooden models hung on the wall, small cardboard models on tables or stands, and large painted models with papier mâché scenery. The loss of faith in architecture has advanced so far in recent years that no image or even building can adequately represent architecture itself: only variety, uncertainty, and incompleteness will do.

Among the models developed after the exhibition and illustrated in this book, Eisenman's House X (fig. 2) is based upon a set of rules which cancel each other out; like a new geometry founded on contradictory axioms, it cannot be understood. The model for it is a three-dimensional representation of an axonometric drawing, which likewise, as Eisenman explains, is self-contradictory. Elsewhere Eisenman has argued that the Nazi holocaust and the nuclear bomb have destroyed the possibility of human control over objects and history, leaving architecture with no task but to symbolize impotence. Looking down on this helpless model, which resembles a crab squashed on a beach, one can only admire Eisenman's success at this task.

Robert A.M. Stern, Eisenman's opposite, has also supplied a representation halfway between a conventional drawing and a conventional model (fig. 3), like a stage set, entirely in keeping with his theatrical notion of a shotgun wedding between Adolf Loos's notorious column for the *Chicago Tribune* competition, and Mies's Chicago prisms. The staginess of Stern's project comes from the preoccupations of Robert Venturi and Charles Moore with facades, signs, and American dreams in Las Vegas and Disneyland. But as usual, Stern fails to achieve either an aura of mystery or suspended belief; he is too anxious to wring wit from Venturi's formula of "complexity and contradiction" to see that it works only when the clashing values are taken seriously.

John Hejduk's model is a fragment of his project "Thirteen Watchtowers of Cannaregio" for Venice. Each tower

1 Staged Gates, *Dayton, Ohio, 1979.*
Mary Miss.

2 *Axonometric model of House X,*
1978. Peter Eisenman.

3 Project *for the new* Chicago Tribune
Tower Competition, 1980. Robert
A.M. Stern. Model.

1

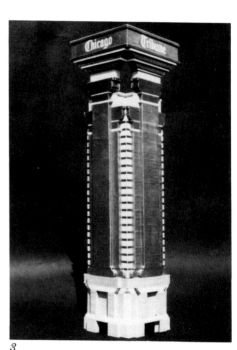

2

11

3

12

4 *Facade studies for French &*
Company, New York, 1978.
Michael Graves.

5 The old city and the new quarters
of Europe, *Luxembourg, 1978.*
Leon Krier.

6 People who live in a circle, *1972.*
Charles Simonds.

7 City of Ausée, *1978. Anne and*
Patrick Poirier. Installation view.

8 Meeting Garden, *Artpark,*
Lewiston, New York, 1980. Siah
Armajani. Painted wood,
11' x 84' x 32'.

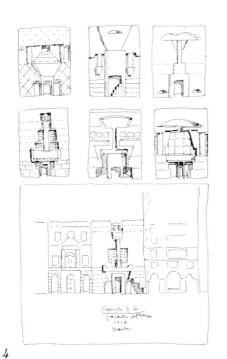

4

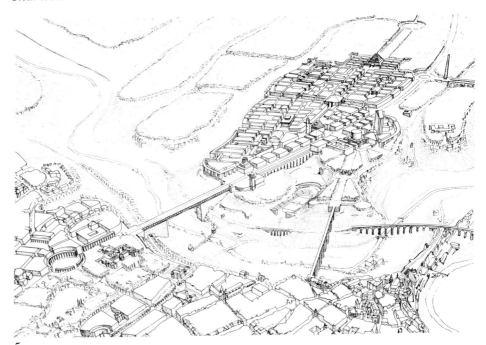

5

6

stands alone, inhabited for life by one man; each floor has its own function. The model, conceived in the format of the secretive shallow cupboards of Joseph Cornell, at once offers and conceals its contents. We look into the cutaway of a tower and out onto an empty piazza, as if looking from the window of a Venetian prison into two other jails, indoors and out: an image of unrelenting stasis, disconnection, and punishment. Yet we never really learn what this tower looks like, neither from this model, nor from the many other renderings of it, just as a lifetime in prison left Silvio Pellico unable to convey in his memoirs the appearance of his dungeons.[1]

The variable position of architecture is most strikingly symbolized by similarity of viewpoints implicit in certain drawings and models. The most important new drawings are views (whereas for the Beaux-Arts they were elevations, for the modernists axonometrics), and among these views many are sweeping bird's-eye panoramas, as in the work of Leon Krier (fig. 5), or thumbnail sketches, as in much of the preliminary; drawing of Michael Graves (fig. 4). In either case, architecture is reduced to a miniature. The spectator stands or soars far above, as powerful as a god; but in his imagination, he shrinks to lilliputian scale to enter these structures. Unlike the great prospects of Le Corbusier, the viewer is invited, even commanded, to inhabit these buildings in his imagination. Graves provides benches for the weary viewer to rest in front of his skyscrapers, Krier elevates statues in his streets for us to measure ourselves against, Rossi gives us a steep incline to mount to a communal grave—whereas with Le Corbusier one never even knows how to cross the street.

The same is true of some sculptures by artists, which have architecture as their ostensible subject: the American Indian structures of Charles Simonds (fig. 6), or especially the ruins of a classical city of Anne and Patrick Poirier (fig. 7), exhibited at the Museum of Modern Art. Of course, models are usually smaller than the buildings they represent, so when can we speak of them as miniatures? It helps if the forms are as small or smaller than our fingertips, the tactile boundary between us and tininess. But some works as large as treehouses, those of Alice Aycock (fig. 9) and Siah Arma-

7

8

Untitled (Medieval Wheel House),
1978. Alice Aycock. Wood, house:
' x 4' x 8'; wheel: 8' diameter.

ani (fig. 8), also seem to be miniatures. What decides is the illusion that the model is inhabitable by our imagination but not by our bodies (so that Aycock leads us to expect access and then denies it). We can never enter the drawings of Le Corbusier, Van Doesburg, Mies, or Eisenman, which are usually shown without people, often without cars, seldom with doors or steps. The works of Simonds, the Poiriers, Aycock, and Armajani, on the other hand, bear the signs of time and effort, reveal the marks of their construction and destruction, show us nooks and crannies where we can enter and hide, and offer us steps to climb, doors to open, and windows to peer out from (as in Rembrandt or in slums and *never* in modern architecture). Just so in the drawings we can feel the damp in the walls of Hejduk's Venice, see the crumbled stone in Graves's quick sketches of Renaissance buildings, and get out of the sun under Krier's colonnades.

What is the meaning or purpose of this ambivalent viewpoint, Olympian and human (or insectile)? I think it can best be referred to a recent observation of Kim Levin's about the current state of art: "Ironically the return to the world can also be seen as an escape. Artists may be merging their work with the discourses of life—making it natural, social, architectural, narrational, theatrical, or ornamental—but they're doing it by turning to fantasy and fiction, to imaginary worlds and private revivals."[2]

The only way now to deal with reality is through the extremes of imagination: the public through the private, the architectural through the pictorial or sculptural, the proximate through the distant. Krier wants to bring us back to Napoleonic or Hadrianic grandeur. Hejduk wants to show us the darkness in the light of the piazzas of Venice. Graves gives us the eternity of the ancient world in the shards of Cubism.

The bifocal viewpoint is really about time, not place. History is the issue now (to a degree that even the most convinced post-modernists failed to anticipate when they invoked it). The question put to history is whether it can offer liberation, in contrast both to the modernist view of it as oppression, and the Marxist dogma of time as predetermina-

tion. Therefore you can return to colonnaded Imperial streets, the towers of Venice, the moldering ruins of Rome, or Neoclassical cemeteries, because in these models and views you still have the sense of hanging back, surveying it all from afar, remaining to the end in command—like putting one toe into the styx.

Notes

1 Silvio Pellico, *Le Mie prigioni* (Turin: 1832), First Edition. Pellico describes a view from his prison room in the Doge's Palace in Venice which is quite similar to the Hejduk model.
2 Kim Levin "The State of the Art: 1980," *College Art Journal* (Fall/Winter, 1980), pp.366-368.

Figure Credits
1, 5, 6, 9 Courtesy of Max Protetch Gallery, New York.
7 Photograph by Rudolph Burckhardt. Collection, Museum of Modern Art, New York.
8 Courtesy of Sonnabend Gallery, New York.
10 Photograph by John A. Ferrari. Courtesy of John Weber Gallery, New York.

The "jealousy" of the model is perhaps most explicit in photographs of models which are virtually indistinguishable from photographs of buildings. The intervention of another form of seemingly motivated representation—namely photography—reinforces the claim to verisimilitude. But the truth of the model does not lie in its referential nature since as simulacrum the model denies the possibilities of its own autonomous objecthood and establishes the building as the ultimate referent, as a reality beyond representation.

It is perhaps the articulation of representation itself which seeks a resuscitation of a "reality" beyond the limits of the sign. In Jean Baudrillard's words, "The sign is haunted by the nostalgia for overcoming its *own* convention, that of being arbitrary. It is haunted by the idea of *total motivation*. It aims at the real as its beyond and abolition. But it cannot jump over its own shadow: this real is produced and reproduced by the sign itself. It is only its *horizon*. Reality is the fantasy by which the sign protects itself indefinitely from the deconstruction that haunts it."[1]

3

Moreover, to think of buildings themselves as only referents, as pure objects, is to overlook their own participation in a process of vision and of language. Buildings too can be seen as representational. To understand a building as a concatenation of similar motifs at different scales—as in a Palladian church facade, is to apply the same mode of representational reading to buildings as is applied to models. The building may also become imprinted with the traces of its own representation. Peter Eisenman's "cardboard architecture" or the buildings of Michael Graves or Aldo Rossi come to represent their own representations. They are at once pictures and buildings.

It is in this reverse current of representation that the critical capacities of the model come into play, exposing architecture's claims to verisimilitude as based on seemingly motivated relationships, on a realism of objects in relation to their meanings and of representation to reality. Peter Eisenman has consistently sought to subvert the workings of representation. Reversing the tricks of model photography, Eisenman emphasized the cardboard qualities of his earlier houses (fig. 5). His recent axonometric models expose the

conventions of axonometric drawing by translating them literally into three-dimensional form (see interview below). The reading of a building as a model or a model as a drawing denies the epistemological fantasies of an architecture that postulates both an object and its adequate representation as its origin or end. Eisenman's deconstructive strategy puts object, process, and representation in unending play.

The play between representation and objecthood has also been of explicit interest in Modernist painting and sculpture. Much of the richness of Modernist pictorial experience lies in our perception of tensions between the actuality of the work as an object and its representational readings—between paint and picture—or else between the object and the artistic activity, as ironically described in Jasper John's ''Fool's House'' (fig. 4). Following the directions indicated by Picasso's guitar, which translated Cubist syntax into actual space (fig. 6), a number of works have situated themselves on the bounds of pictorialism and objecthood, locating the concerns of art at a crossroad of painting, sculpture, and architecture. In the planar construction of Russian avant-garde art, for example, the discovery of the surface and objecthood of painting intersects with the investigation of the pictorial nature of the wall to open a space in which the visual and the physical maintain an uneasy balance. This planar dimension might be considered similar to the space of the model. In Ivan Puni's relief (fig. 7), a Cubist pictorial syntax becomes a redundant supplement to actual physical form. But the shallow space of the relief and the composition of the construction are themselves spatial translation of developments in avant-garde painting. In this meeting-space of actuality and representation (which is, incidentally, flattened and obscured by photography), the most ideal conception coexists with an affirmation of the absolute materiality of the object. It allows ideas to become models. As in collage, the real becomes, to some extent, representational, and the representational real.

El Lissitzky's Proun Room (fig. 8) and Piet Mondrian's studio (fig. 9) might then be considered full-scale models, responding perhaps to Suarez Miranda's criteria. They announce a new relationship between painting, sculpture, and

4 Fool's House, *1962. Jasper Johns.*
Oil on canvas with objects, 72" x 36".

5 *House II, Hardwick, Vermont,*
1968. Peter Eisenman.

architecture, in which works of art are no longer contained within exhibition spaces but become continuous with them.

The stage is another privileged locus for a convergence between actual and representational space. Scenography is one of the margins of architecture in which the bounds between picture and object are effaced, and this conjunction might also afford us some understanding of the workings of the model. In the Teatro Olimpico (figs. 10, 11), built to the designs of Palladio and Scamozzi, the spaces of illusion, of Classical recall, and of actuality are united through perspective, and the theater and the city are integrated as two aspects of a single paradigm. The Teatro constitutes a strategy for the renovation of the city, through an introspective transformation of the city into a theater. Once within the theater the *frons scenae* opens up onto a "street scene" in which perspectival representation literalizes a realm lying somewhere between actuality and illusion. This, perhaps, is the space of the model. The street scene can be entered, yet its recession is rapidly foreshortened, so that its representational perspectivalism is destroyed by the intrusion of the subject.

Palladio's theater finds a contemporary counterpart in Rossi's floating theater in Venice, which transforms the actual city into theater (fig. 12). In this case, the Teatro del Mondo is a full-scale model, but a model nonetheless: its juxtaposition with the church of Santa Maria della Salute underscores its representational relationship to the city, and while it is large enough to contain plays inside it, its real stage is clearly outside. At a smaller scale, Rossi's *Teatrino Scientifico* (frontispiece) returns the city to the space of the model. Within the theater there is an implied continuity between the foreground "models" of the Galaratese and the receding backdrop of the Modena cemetery. This exemplifies that preoccupation with the nature of representation in drawings, models, and buildings which is Rossi's obsessive concern. Rossi's work continuously presents and represents. His analogical enterprise, like Surrealism, juxtaposes the "real" and the imaginary, allowing for a continual interplay, a constant substitution. And like Surrealism, his work foils any attempt to find a resting point in the real.

6

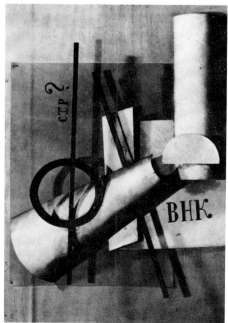

7

6 Guitar, *1912. Pablo Picasso. Metal with wire.*

7 *Sculpture reconstructed from a 1916 drawing of the 1915 original. Ivan Puni. Partially painted wood, tin, and cardboard, 30" x 19" x 3".*
The Puni relief actualizes in three dimensions *a Cubist composition. In addition, the shading on the volumes is painted. In the photograph the tensions caused by the redundancy are lost, and the painted shadows seem real.*

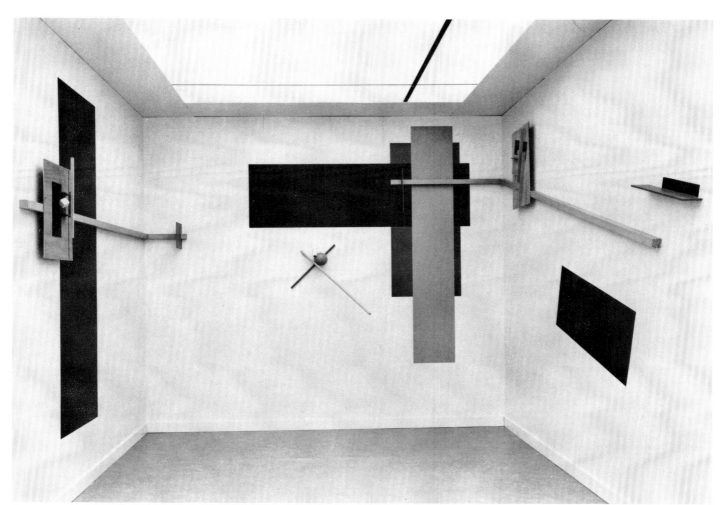

8

9

8 Prounroom, *Berlin, 1923. El Lissitzky. Installation view of reconstruction at the Solomon R. Guggenheim Museum, 1979. Painted wood, 118" x 118" x 102".*

9 The Paris Studio, *1926. Piet Mondrian.*

24 *10 Teatro Olimpico, Venice,
1579-1584. Andrea Palladio and
Vincenzo Scamozzi. Model.*

11 Teatro Olimpico.

*12 Teatro del Mondo. Venice
Biennale, 1979-1980. Aldo Rossi.*

10

11

26 *13 Facade for Strada Novissima,*
Venice Biennale, 1980.
Hans Hollein.

13

Yet the classical theater has a tradition of posing as a simulacrum of reality, in which the theater's theatricality lies in its play for the spectator, in its demand for willing suspension of disbelief without disclosing its fictional nature. At the most recent Venice Biennale, entitled *The Presence of the Past,* the theatrical capacities of the model and its potential for historical mystification were only occasionally subverted by the model's critical potential. The Strada Novissima purported to represent both the urban interventions of the Renaissance—as in the Strada Nuova in Genoa—and their theatrical counterparts—as in the Teatro Olimpico. But in this confusion of City and Theater, "history" repeats tragedy in the form of farce. Like the recent repetition of the Chicago Tribune Competition, the "Post-Modern" nostalgia underlying this exhibition glorified the lulling promise of the simulacrum. The Strada Novissima, built by the technicians of *Cinecittà,* was a triumph of scenographic delusion.

Leon Krier's insistence upon *real* materials in his segment can be seen as the most deluded of all in its denial of the inherent representationalism of the model. On the other hand, the suspension of disbelief insisted on by Krier was undermined in Hans Hollein's sardonic exploitation of the dual capacity of the model as both object and representation. Loos's Tribune Tower proposal of 1922 parodied the iconographic and proportional problems of the skyscraper by identifying them with those of the "primary sign" of architecture, the column. Hollein's "quotation" of Loos (fig. 13) is a scale model of the skyscraper which also happens to be the size of a column. It situates the history of architecture within a broken syntagm, between nature and culture, and like Loos, makes denial the strongest affirmation.

In the world of Borgesian imagination, Suarez Miranda turns out to be as much of a fiction as the Empire he visited. Borges's quotation is finally revealed as a "quotation," a writing ironically disguised as reading. Through this oblique device Borges reminds us of our own demands for a history whose problematic is not so different from that of the model. A history permeated by nostalgia, which seeks to recuperate a lost origin of architecture, can only succeed in denying the conditions of its own making. Like the theater

and the simulacrum, it can only demand the suspension of our disbelief in order to distract and compensate for the loss of a genuine sense of historicity. It seeks to deny its own presence by a mystification in the name of the real, and proposes history as a book, open for perusal and quotation, without admitting that history is in the writing.

Notes
1 Jean Baudrillard, *Pour une Economie Politique du Signe* (Paris: Gallimard, 1973), p.189. Translation by author.
2 Jorge Luis Borges, "Of Exactitude in Science" in *A Universal History of Infamy* (New York: E.P. Dutton, 1979).

Figure Credits
Frontispiece by Giacinta Manfredi.
3 Reprinted from *Bramante* by Arnaldo Bruschi, Thames and Hudson, London.
4 Courtesy of Leo Castelli Galley, New York.
5 Photograph by Norman McGrath.
7 Reprinted from Planes, The Soloman R. Guggenheim Museum, New York.
8 Photograph by Robert E. Mates. Courtesy of The Solomon R. Guggenheim Museum, New York.
13 Photograph by Antonio Martinelli.

Idea as Model 1976

House Without Rooms

Raimund Abraham

30   The fragmented elements of the house,
archaic by their own nature,
become inseparably compressed
within a fragile cosmology,
denying the conquest of habitation,
unless space is stripped of its
Euclidean dimension.
Then the House is virtually born:
submerged and erect,
receiving and rejecting,
fertile with sediments of unknown
intimacy.

Horizons appear tilted, verticalized.
Strips of sky are buried in shadows
of the earth's crust.
Gravity looses its eternal dominance.
Light is filtered through stairs
toward the inner parts of the House,
barely illuminating motionless landscapes of flesh and stone: fossils of
an unchallenged present.

The inner silence remains protected
by the armor of the outer walls,
metallic reminiscence of ancient
shelters.

The Elements become the House itself,
transformed into simultaneous
projections of Room, Window,
Wall, Sky, Earth, Stair, Door.
And with this total fusion
of objects and sensations,
bodies are transmuted forms.

*Folding is, with regard to
the large printed leaf,
an almost religious sign:
which is not as striking
as its packing together,
in thickness, offering in-
deed, the soul's minute tomb.*
Quant au Livre, *Stéphane Mallarmé*

House Without Rooms. *Two views.*
Wood with metallic paint.

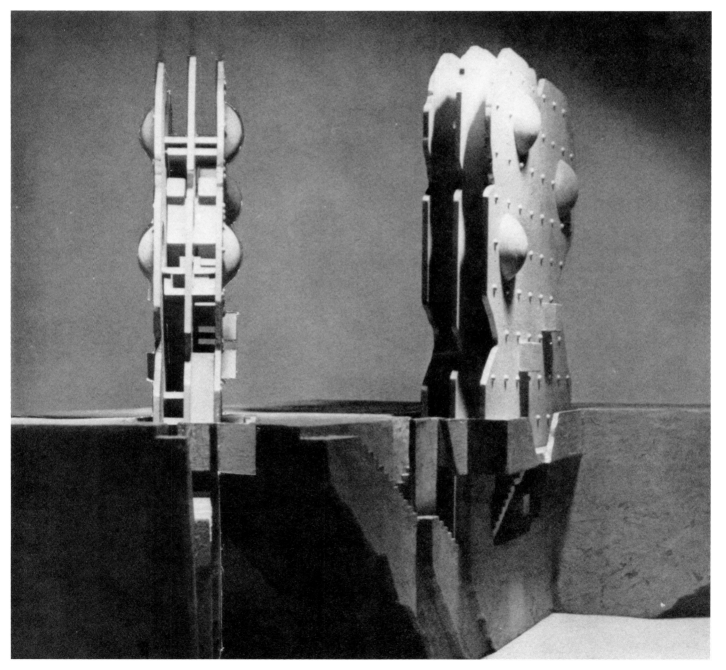

Les Echelles: House for a Musician in Majorca

Diana Agrest

House for a Musician in Majorca, 1975. Analytic model. Plexiglass, paint, lit from within.

Model assistant: Chris Barron

32 This entire house is conceived as a public object, a cultural event utilizing the rarely exploited public potential of the house. Groups of musicians and actors could be set on the various terraces as well as along the staircase; the house would become a kind of stage.

The reading that is thereby produced is not a linear discourse but an infinite and spatialized text.

This theatrical vehicle exists as a sequence of "gardens" or fragments of gardens, ranging from the elements of nature to the abstract grid of culture, organized along different modes of transition: staircase, bridges, doors, passageway.

The site is a hillside overlooking the Mediterranean Sea. The house is conceived not just as a private interior space, but also as a building which has an outside life of its own; it is therefore like two buildings which may be experienced independently or as interrelated.

The glass-block staircase provides access to the house and also to the terraces. The staircase illuminated from within at night like a cascade of light emphasizes the dramatic, public aspect. It establishes a dynamic connection with the hillside, which is set in a dialectical relationship with the static platform. The top of the staircase becomes one of the house's significant places, from which one may watch the sunset, reflect, or play music.

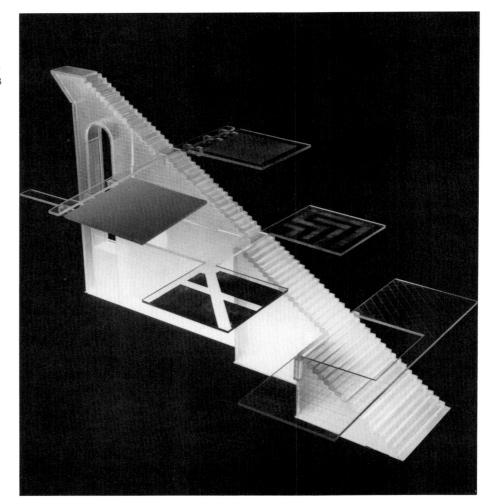

Architecture Between Memory and Amnesia

Diana Agrest
Mario Gandelsonas

Proposal for a Suburban Center in Minneapolis. Model. Plexiglass, cardboard, wood, paint.

Proposal For a Suburban Center in Minneapolis—On The Edge Of The Mississippi River

Design is reading. Design is rewriting existent architecture. Design is transforming existent types; both architectural and urban, both building and place types. Design implies a dialectic between the new in relation to the *memory* of the old. But design is also a *production of meaning,* the transformation of the old into the new; the mutation of the known into the unknown. Design is also amnesia; the loss of memory as a possibility for invention.

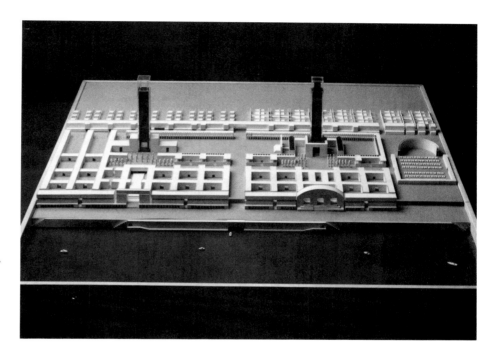

This project explores these theses through the relationship between urban and suburban realms. First, the typologies which characterize the sparse suburban landscape and are not yet part of the memory of architecture. Second, the juxtaposition of European density with suburbia to create another kind of space; the one contaminating the other and vice versa. New forms and meanings arise when the urban and the suburban interact and contradict each other; for example, when public places are incorporated into the private house.

The east bank of the Mississippi River in Minneapolis comprises a gridded suburban sprawl unrelated to the river. This typical American grid fails to provide for any inflection of the city by the river and vice versa. The project introduces variety by breaking the grid, through the fragmentation and superimposition of various scales within the grid. We introduced a superblock grid, a smaller scale grid, suburban grid, and a grid configurating a space which is neither urban nor suburban, consisting of quadrangles of courtyard housing where the street is replaced by small squares. The new urban grid is modelled as a sequence of public spaces and high rises that function as monuments which punctuate the urban space the way obelisks do in the classical city. The skyscrapers also act like lighthouses—signs which transform the symbolism of the unique monument into an empty center, a street which does not lead anywhere, a text which dissolves architectural language.

34 Diagrammatic synthesis of six
transformations. The results of these
transformations:
   Red
   Orange
   Yellow
   Blue
   Dark Blue
Warm colors show transformations
in section that are marked in plan.

Cool colors show transformations in
plan that are marked in elevation.

Translucent blocks mark volumes of
space that are a residue of actual
solids and as such are given an order,
definition, and positive quality.

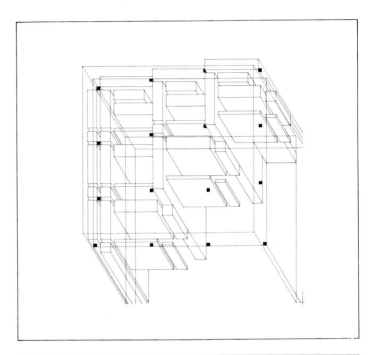

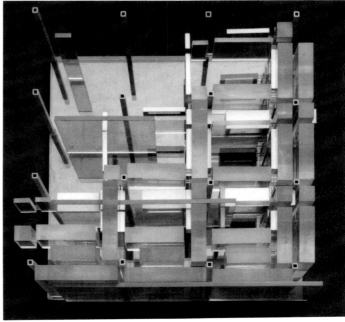

House II Transformations.
Plexiglass, paint.

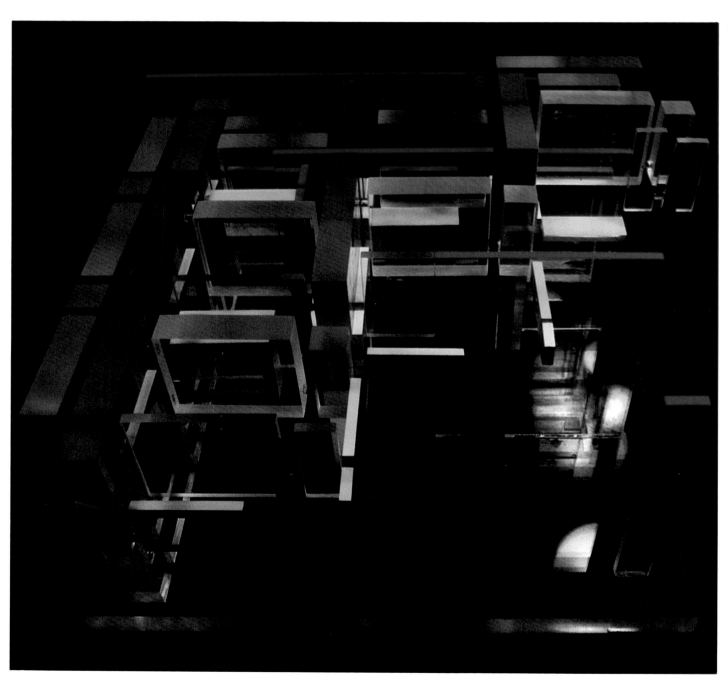

Competition for the New French Embassy in Washington, D.C.

Anthony Eardley
Guillermo Jullian De La Fuente
Alfred Koetter

36 The three architects prepared a sequence of study sketches, collages, and constructions of problems generated by the complex program of the competition for the new French Embassy in Washington, D.C.

First there was an articulation of the spatial and circulatory functions within the basic square unit. By reference to Jullian's previous experiences in structuring an embassy program for the French Embassy in Brasilia, this program was subjected to arithmetical analysis in order to precisely determine the lowest common spatial denominator of the specified areas.

The second model was a three-dimensional, polychromatic collage employing a modified basic square unit. This model permitted us to identify the problems inherent in unit rotation, differential elevations, and positive/negative residues.

There was then an exploration of the three-dimensional structure of the basic square unit. At this point our intuition that the lowest common denominator of the plan might be reutilized in the section was confirmed.

The further development of these spatial explorations took form in a chipboard and papier-mâché model and a hypothetical model of a parking system, among others.

The Wageman House and the Crooks House

Michael Graves

38 Once we have modeled or represented an idea, that representation, the object made, begins to have a life of its own, somewhat separate from or beyond our original conception. The new life of the physical object then conditions further ideas and thoughts in a process of development.

I find this interchange between idea and artifact to have the capacity to embrace phenomena outside itself and to allow us to broaden the intensity of the idea through memory and thoughts of things past. The spirit of invention could be said to occur between the reciprocity of thought and object. It is not a matter of translation; it is a matter of a continuing reciprocity between thought and object. The tension of lines on paper or cardboard in space has an insistence of its own that describes possibilities which perhaps could not be imagined in thought alone.

If various aspects of a whole are fragmented or isolated in model form, the model can be seen as a conceptual condition, a detail, or an idea which is given importance by its isolation. By virtue of this isolation, we more clearly see not only the separable life of that piece but also how it involves aspects of the whole within it.

The Wageman House, because of its context, is not seen in the round. Adjacent buildings restrict the appreciation of the object as a figure in the landscape and require, because of the primary street facade, a frontal ac-

cess to the building. The primacy of the street facade has an insistence in the conception of the house which is not shared by other sides. It was my intention in isolating the front facade of the building to describe, in part on that face, the idea of movement or procession through the building and to suggest in that frontal plane a foreground (the preceding space, the lawn in front of the facade), a middle ground (the facade itself), and a background (the space behind the face). There was an attempt to bring the green of the horizontal plane in front of the facade into the face itself so as more firmly to root it in the ground. This was achieved by a forcing of the perspective of the green into the rusticated base course of the facade itself.

There was also an attempt to suggest the space or room behind the facade by another perspectival gesture, a succession of window planes. In both the Wageman House and the Crooks House, the facade studies become representations of surfaces which presume the void or room in front and in back of them. The plane of the architectural facade, like a painting, can thus be studied three-dimensionally, since it is possible to perceive foreground and background through the datum provided by the middle ground of the facade. In study, the facade becomes a series of surfaces, creating voids which become architectural spaces. In this way, the model represents a study of facades and surface planes, of illusionistic rather than real space.

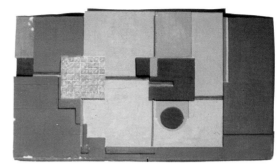

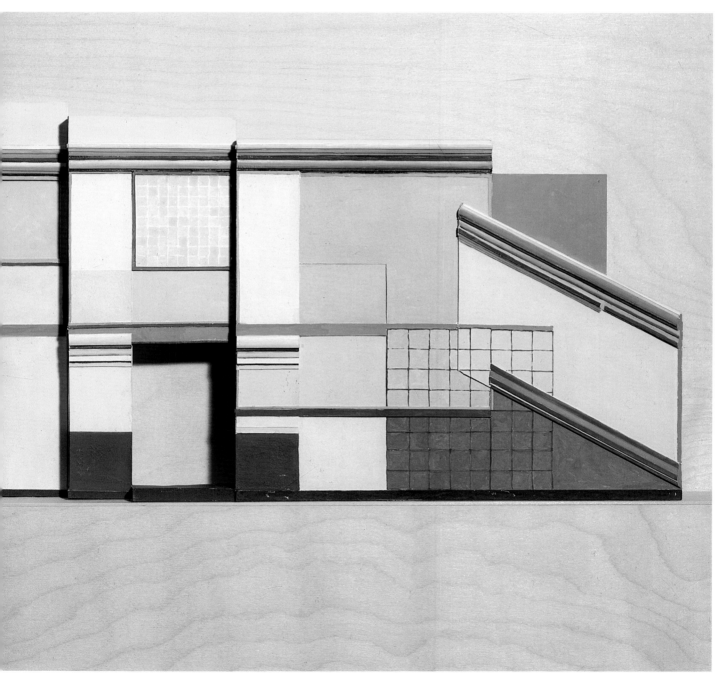

Band-Aid

William Ellis

40 This model is an ideogram of a proposal made for downtown Minneapolis. The problem was to create a backdrop for several free-standing urban objects sitting in a vast open space: a railroad station, a new circus-like skating rink, and several existing commercial and apartment buildings. It proposes the application of a continuous facade about ten feet in depth onto the face of three existing blocks at the edge of the open space.

The facade consolidates the three blocks, changing—without interfering with—the existing conditions. In addition, it acts as both a new object and a non-object, as both a one-sided object and a two-sided object. As such it seams together two open spaces—the field behind the three blocks and the piazza in front, and it distinguishes the front piazza as preferred and the field behind as inferior.

The narrow, continuous space forms a covered pedestrian way at grade level, an enclosed all-weather "skyway" for pedestrians at the second level, and balconies for the offices behind at the upper levels.

Model: Liviu Dimitriu
Assistant: Michael Miller

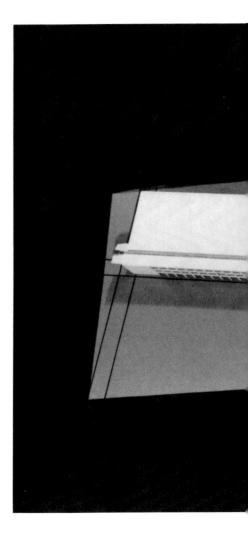

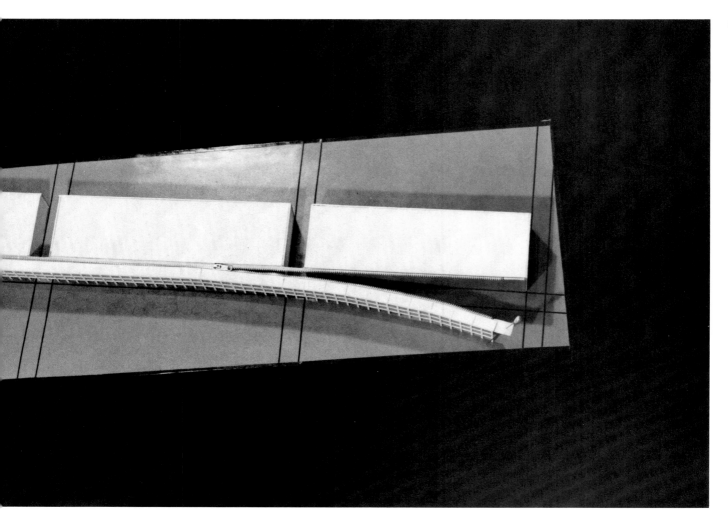

John Hejduk

42 Three study models
of Bye House
plus one of
"Third Wall House."

The center model
of Bye studies
indicates possibility of
"rendering a house."

Openings in walls
are sectional cuts
which permit movement
from one void
to another void:
Void
Solid
Void
to make voids
dense without solidifying.

Top: Bye House. Model.

Bottom: Three study models, Bye House. One study model, "Third Wall House." Mixed media.

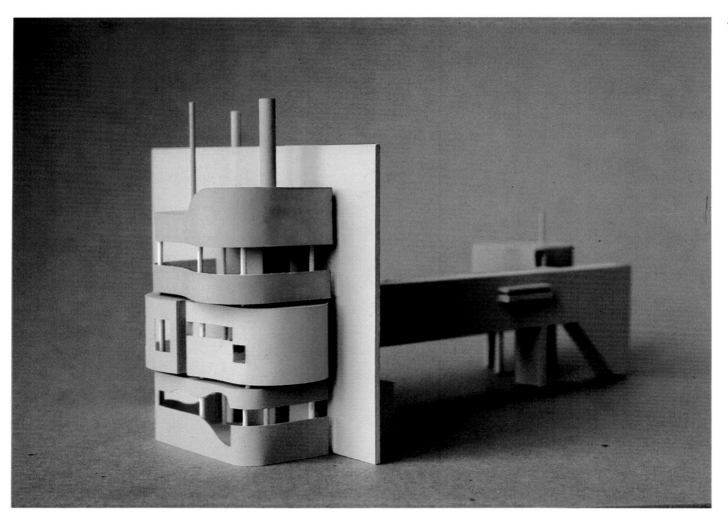

Godhouse

Amancio Guedes

Godhouse. *Carved wood.*

Right: Godhouse. *Plan.*

44   Temple as toy. Model of an idea.
One of a family of five similar
Godhouses carved from the trunk of
a *figus lirata* that grew too big in the
entrance to the Smiling Lion.

Temple breaking up into seven
buildings. Seven hermetic roofs sup-
ported by seventeen columns and
three walls in six kinds of cir-
cumstances.

Building as both space-trap and object in space—to be seen from all
sides, including from the hovering
position and from below the
hypothetical floor in the old-fashioned
manner of a Choisy drawing.

Godhouse in the no-man's-land between the territories of sculpture and
architecture.

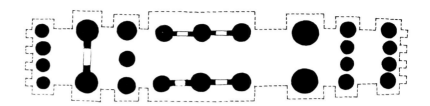

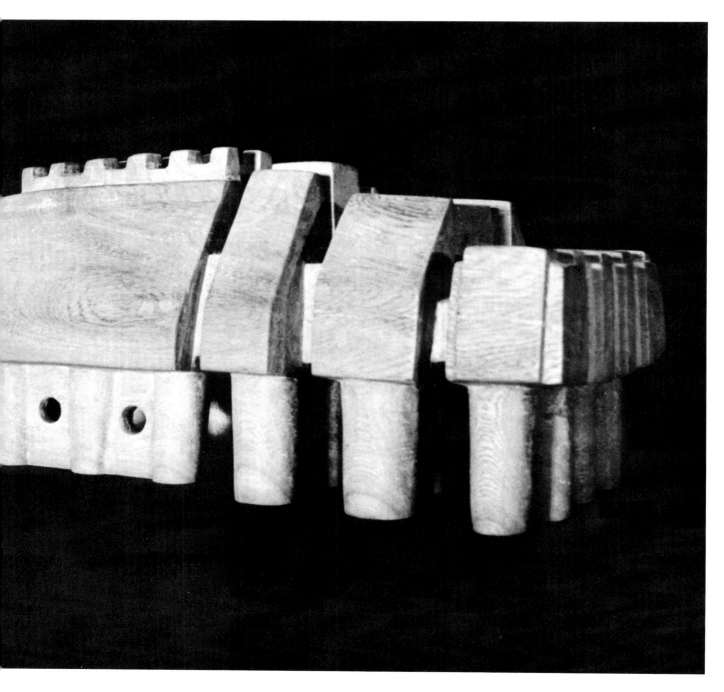

Gwathmey Residence and Studio

**Gwathmey and Henderson
Architects**

46 *Site*
One-acre field with ocean view on southern shore of Long Island.

Program
Residence and studio for painter and textile designer.

Construction
Slab on grade, wood frame, cedar siding (exterior and interior).

The Despair of Janus

Leon Krier
Massimo Scolari

48   For a very long time, Massimo
Scolari and Leon Krier talked almost
affectionately about the idea of a
possible collaboration. But avoiding
the abysmal difficulty of such an
enterprise, we decided instead to
describe somewhat enthusiastically
the relationship which some of our
buildings have.

Four Spatial Transformations of a Grid

Bernhard Leitner

50   A three-dimensional (neutral) grid of loudspeakers distributed in space is the instrument-like condition for creating various architectures of sound. In architectures of sound the spaces are shaped by programmed motions of sound. The model illustrates four transformations of the grid: 1. swinging space—a pendulum-like motion; 2. vertical space—sound descending vertically (crescendo) and moving upward again (decrescendo); 3. sound tube—a vertically circling motion; 4. space composition *IV*— a free delination with varying sounds and speeds. Through repetition these spatial situations are extended in time.

Four Spatial Transformations of a Grid. *Model. Plexiglass, paint.*

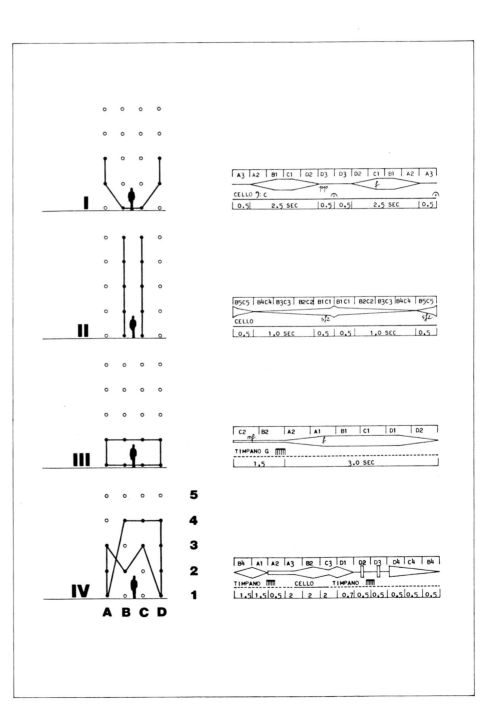

Fountain House

Rodolfo Machado
Jorge Silvetti

52 The Fountain House, which was designed in 1975 as a second residence for an artist couple in Southern California, was partially the result of our concern with three topics derived from our critical position on architecture. These can be summarized as follows:

1. Architecture without guilt. We believe that it is essential to liberate the architect's mind from some paralyzing guilt feelings concerning the elaboration of form. This liberating effort has the result of reintroducing into architecture the notions of seduction, eroticism, and pleasure (the designer's through creation and the beholder's through the perception of forms).

2. Architecture through progressive elitism rather than through reactionary populism. Current populist attempts are paradoxically rooted in a paternalistic, reactionary position that seeks to produce "give 'em what they want" rather than creatively transform the environment.

3. Architecture as a polyphonic object. In our projects we have been evolving a design technique that generates an effect that we call dispersion of sense throughout the building. This technique, which consists of a set of rhetorical operations performed upon different vocabularies, is opposed to other manners of formalization that produce monosemic, "flat" buildings. For this metaphorical quality formal traits should attain relative dominance and the parts should be made interdependent; the designer should know how to stop short of the completion of a motif in order to interrupt a particular polyphonic reading so as to allow it to blend, in turn, with another.

These objectives have led us to rediscover some lost methodologies (which have been left unexplored since the days of Piranesi and Sir John Soane), such as a method of composition that utilizes fragments of architectures. We believe that the final result recovers some essential elements of the architectural experience, particularly the pleasure given by a set of highly conscious operations.

Fountain House. Model. Cardboard,
paint.

53

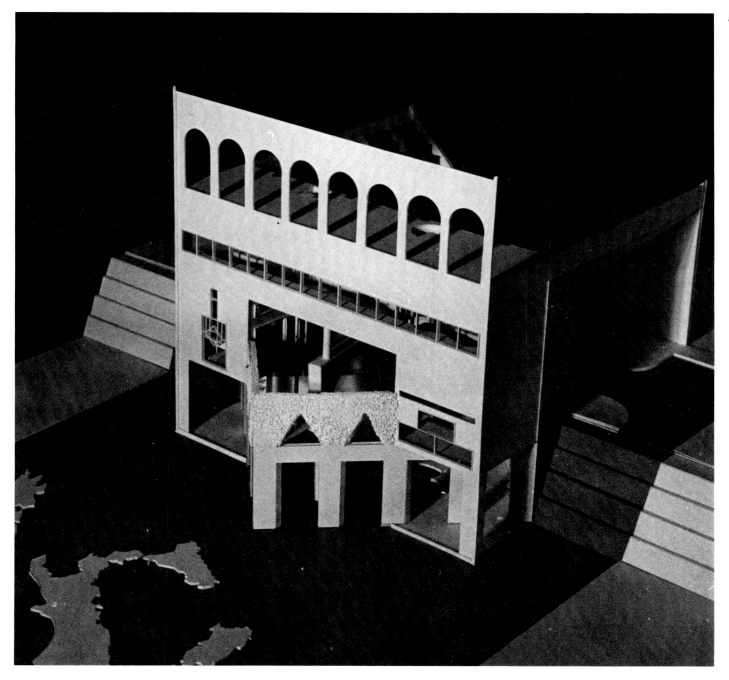

House in Pound Ridge

Richard Meier

54 Approached by a long driveway through an avenue of trees, this transparent pavilion in a country setting partakes of and is extended into nature through its glass skin. But the lucid envelope belies qualities of luxury and mystery that are purely spatial in derivation and occur within a structural framework of rigorous physical and intellectual simplicity.

Twelve steel columns, regularly spaced, pierce the three–story volume from top to bottom. Within this cage of steel there are no walls, but the space acquires interior definition around the encapsulated form of the master bedroom, which hovers under the roof, looking out to the sky.

In contrast to this spatial richness is the cloistered simplicity of the entrance side whose closed white walls are self-supporting. From outside it may be seen as a form entering the high volume under the roof. Within are service spaces at ground level, and above, two skylit bedrooms opening to the interior through a glazed gallery under twin-walled roof gardens, which also look to a high interior space.

Thus the closed rooms are linked visually by this view to the center, and the central space is diffused throughout, and extended beyond its transparent physical boundaries to the encircling trees. At night the trees are lit, and in the splendid isolation of the site there is a view of stars and the somber shadows of trees.

House in Pound Ridge, New York, 1969. Model. Cardboard, plexiglass, wood.

A Study of a Wall With Windows

Rafael Moneo

56   Architectural models have traditionally been connected with the
three-dimensional representation of
built architecture through a reduction
of scale. The aim of our proposal is to
avoid the problems of change in scale
by admitting the possibility of
materializing the drawing into three
dimensions. The convention of the
drawing acquires its own reality in
this way.

An axonometric drawing of a wall
therefore becomes a real volume, a
three-dimensional object, thus reversing the standard operation of reduc-
ing a three-dimensional object to a
two-dimensional representation. The
direction of the forty-five degree
angle that the axonometric drawing
introduces becomes frozen in the
volume of the model, imprisoning our
vision, in spite of its corporeality, the
model can be seen only in a single
way—a situation that contradicts the
new volumetric condition of the
drawing.

Study of the facade of Bankinter, a building in Madrid designed by Ramon Bescos and Rafael Moneo. Cardboard.

A House Near New York

Charles Moore
Richard Oliver

58 The clients for this house near New York were a man who had recently lost his sight and his sighted wife and children. To enable the client to be fully involved as a participant in the design of his house, we used vacuum-formed bas-relief plans, which we call vacu-drawings. The client would read the vacu-drawings linearly, like a musical composition (or like the Gutenberg Bible), moving his hands from room to room to learn the shape of his house, and discovering the places where movement seemed easy or disorienting. The process is unlike that used by the typical sighted client, who generally views a plan or model as a whole gestalt, often accompanied by a simplified response such as "wow!" or "ugh."

The client's sighted wife also found the vacu-drawings useful in understanding the house. The raised walls, together with the indications of doors, windows, stairs, and counters, provided the sense of three-dimensional reality missing from two-dimensional plans (which she, quite typically for a lay person, found abstract and difficult to read). The vacu-drawings allowed her, and other members of the family, to envision the various rooms as actual places.

A typical mold for a vacu-drawing is made of chipboard and balsa wood. The vacu-drawings were produced in a warming oven connected to a vacuum pump (an arrangement reminiscent of Rube Goldberg, and created by William Grover at the Factory in Essex, Connecticut.

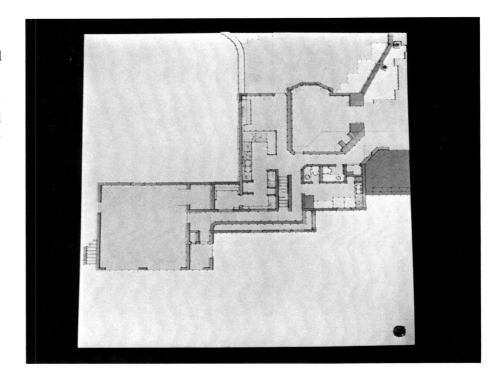

A House near New York. Model.
Chipboard, balsa wood, plastic.

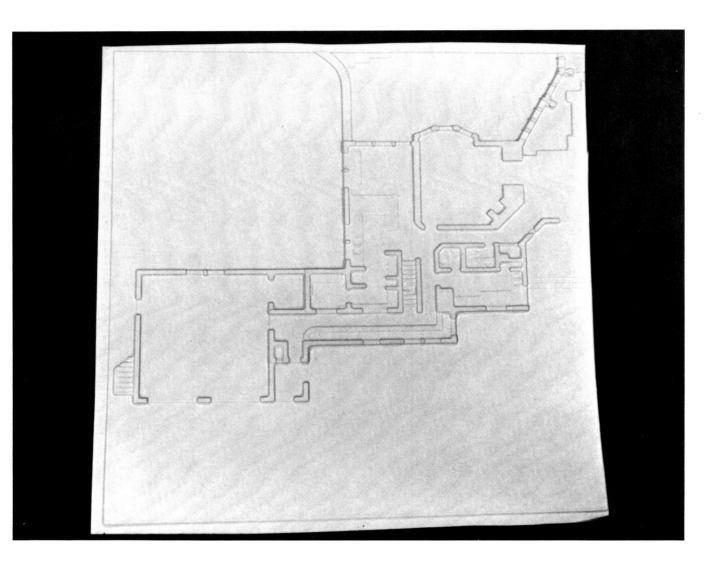

Madden House I

Jaquelin Robertson

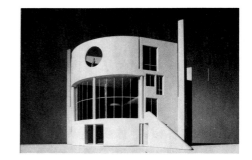

60 This house, intended as centerpiece for a famous Kentucky horse farm, is an evocation of the legendary Southern "great house" a formal response to existing site, programmatic, and cultural conditions through the interaction of modern and classical architectural vocabulary.

The little model we made is forced to play two different roles: one to portray the object, the other to try to represent physically *ideas* about the object that go beyond its physicality. So the model has to be both tiny twin and symbolic surrogate. It says: "Look at me, I am literal with respect to a generalized form, but I'm also a liar, an imposter. For I can't really ever be an exact reproduction, but only representative of specific architectural devices." The model, that is, is certainly not a "little house." Its reduced scale has an amended meaning and purpose. While it *can* condense and elaborate some of its original's ultimate aesthetic quality, both abstract and cultural, it can only *suggest* this in general terms. It suffers, then, from being a toy which wants to be much more, yet cannot be; wants to be icon and "real" at the same time; wants to be true when it involves no "building," no construction. Yet still this toy remains a serious and telling kind of play; *real* make-believe with respect to pattern and order.

This model makes its attempt to illustrate some of the concerns at work: the symmetry of front and back and at the same time their geometric dissimilarities and separation from one another (each side performing, as it does, a different site function—something not apparent in the neutral context of the model); the detail-less, "modern" nature of certain "classical" elements (columns, pediments, oculus windows); the differences between old kinds of openings which are not glazed (e.g. the oculus) and new kinds of doors and windows; the classical tripartite sectional organization—solid base, glazed and gaping parterre drum, semi-permeable upper story—counterpointing the pulled apart and rotated plan form; the "inside" space which is outside on the roof and the "outside" space of the great hall—part of the meadow beyond—which is enclosed; the formal second-floor porch counterpointing the open fourth-floor sundeck; and so forth.

The model narrates all these ideas; yet finally and most tellingly, it is about itself as an *idea scaffold for the real thing,* about the "essence" of certain future intentions, about formal structure and conceptual density. A loaded toy.

Madden House I, 1967. Model.
Cardboard, plexiglass, wood.

New York Townhouse

Robert A. M. Stern

62   The design of this new street facade connects with the classicist architecture of the much taller apartment buildings at its flanks. In response to the problems of scale implicit in this anomalous situation, a number of strategies have been employed. First, references on the facade to the real sizes and positions of the elements in the plan and section have been played down in favor of allusions to the base/shaft/capital schema of the taller buildings: Second, there are intimations of vestigial pilasters at the edges, and a gradual progression in the vertical plane is established. Finally, the whole is capped by a cornice which appears to be suspended from above. These strategies help connect the facade with the form-language of its neighbors and evoke images of traditional and classicist townhouse design.

New York Townhouse. Model.
Cardboard, plexiglass, wood.

Animal Crackers

Stanley Tigerman

64 The minimum house of the suburbs
has for some time visually been
thought of as married to man's notion of nature. "Animal Crackers" is
an attempt to tie that minimal statement to the vehicle that necessarily
moves man to and from the suburbs
rather than to natural forms. As such
it is thought of as a calliope-like vehicle whose form and coloration in
primaries stand in opposition to
nature. Being minimal, it suggests
cutouts through color change without
actually having pierced surfaces. Its
baked enamel metal farm siding in
profile implies a car backed up onto
the land and fixed forever in the
forest.

Animal Crackers. *Cardboard, paint.*

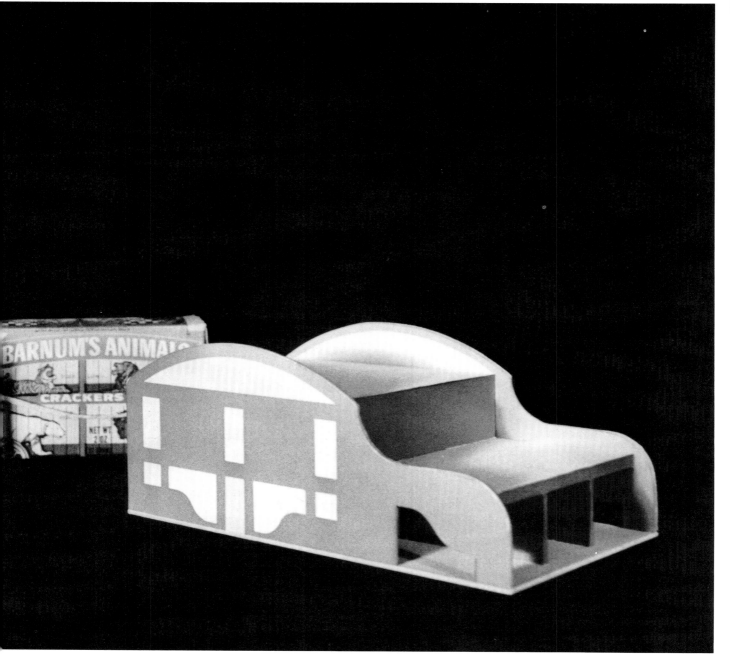

**Morphology of the Cube
(An Extract)**

O.M. Ungers

66 When man consciously took an isolated, clearly defined area from indefinite, unlimited open space, and demarcated this area—be it only with a gesture—he created an architectural space. This gesture initiates an intellectual dialogue with the environment.

By using the simple form of the cube one might demonstrate three basic concepts of spatial formation. The cube can be represented by three elements: first, linear elements defining the corners; second, planar elements defining the different planes of the cube; third, volumetric elements determining the space in between. Linear elements are posts, beams, pilotis, edges, while the planar elements are ceiling panels, boards, and slabs. The volumetric elements are building blocks, cubes, and enclosed spaces.

The space–defining elements of a volume do not necessarily concern the space as an enclosure. They deal only with the boundaries, the edges, and the external determinants of the space. The volume relates to the sculptural aspect of architecture: the formation of space, the architectural component. It includes the space between the volumes. The volume is the positive element, creating forms; the space in between is the negative element, the form-receiving part of architecture.

The first stage of spatial formation beyond the basic geometric volume of the cube consists of a regular repetition of similar parts as demonstrated in the model. In reality, the principle of repetition applies to the addition of a series of equal rooms or the regular growth of cellular patterns.

Higbie House

**Tod Williams and Associates,
Architects**

68 This 1/8 inch scale model is the third
one made of this house, which was
designed for a large open site in the
northwest. The overriding idea of the
house was to superimpose two
structures; one structure to
represent the needs of the owners—a
wood and glass structure of modest
scale. The other to represent the
site—steel and stone shielding the
snow and sun, and addressing the
power of the open range.

Model: George Raustiallia

Higbie House. Model. Cardboard,
plexiglass, paint, wood.

Et in Arcadia Ego

Stuart Wrede

70 A cube of earth reinforced inside with wood frame and wire mesh is seeded with grass. The grass is watered and clipped regularly. The piece may be seen as a prototype for a new landscape art. "Et in Arcadia Ego" is also a hommage to Adolf Loos.

This model is one of three (see other model on page 117) which are in the tradition of non-utilitarian architecture, whose function is symbolic only; that of the folly, gateway, fountain or monument. They were meant to give pleasure or amuse, to act as symbols and to conjure up myths but seldom to be used for any practical purpose. The Modern Movement with its emphasis on the utilitarian and the functional, its shunning of myth, symbol, pleasure and pain, put an end to this tradition. We have suffered its absence for over fifty years, repressing our innate need to articulate in three dimensions vital spiritual, cultural, and emotional symbols. This denial which has taken place under the banner of functionalism, empiricism, and economy will surely be regarded as one of the truly perverse cultural manifestations of the twentieth century.

On another level we must revitalize the symbolic meaning of plant material such as ivy and grass which in their conventional usage by the wider culture have sunk to the level of clichés. By using such material in new contexts and recombinations we may once again begin to unlock the primal sensuality and symbolism inherent in them.

Et in Arcadia Ego. *Earth, wood frame, wire mesh, grass.*

Idea as Model 1976

Figure Credits
*All models in the 1976 exhibition, except those designated below,
were photographed by Judith Turner.*
p. 38 Photograph by Dick Frank
p. 43 Photograph by Keat Tan
pp. 64,65 Photographs by Ed Stoecklein

71

Idea as Model 1980

City of Twofold Vision

Raimund Abraham

74   A rectangular grid based on a building module of 2.50 meters is superimposed on the amorphous fabric of existing open areas and indigenous non-historic buildings. The geometric "imprints" of these buildings remain to provide the foundations of new structures, while the collision of these elements with the proposed architectonic elements form the dialectical principle of the total architectural composition.

Along the main north = south axis of the compositional field three sequentially ordered square blocks form the compositional, functional, and symbolic core of the new city fragment. A network of perpendicular linear blocks and passages radiates from the central squares toward the periphery of the site, interconnecting the cores.

Their symmetrical pattern is interrupted and distorted by the irregular formations of existing canals, walls, and buildings.

Toward the historic edges of the Cannaregio Canal on the east and the Grand Canal on the south, they merge organically with the existing historic buildings, while toward the lagoon on the north and the railroad station on the west they are terminated by definite architectural boundaries.

The sequence of the three squares reveals a progressive change from a fragmented composition toward an idealized geometric, spatial condition.

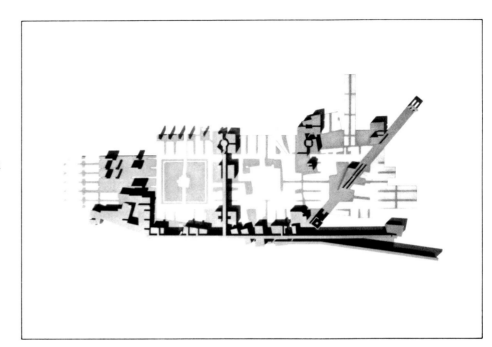

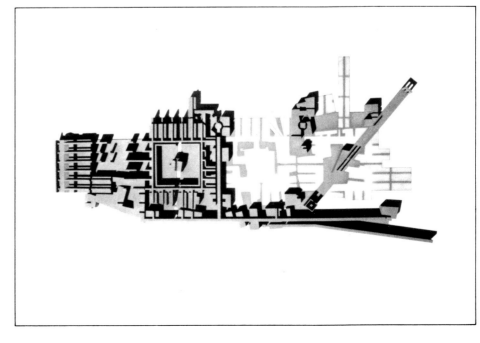

City of Twofold Vision, *1978-1980.*
Model. Project for the Venice
Biennale.

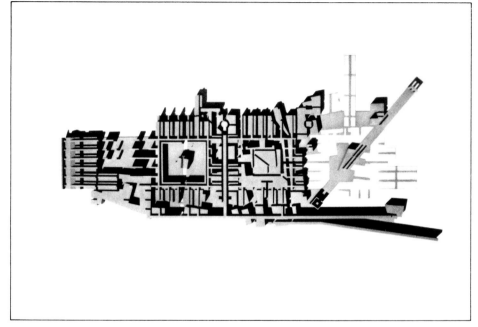

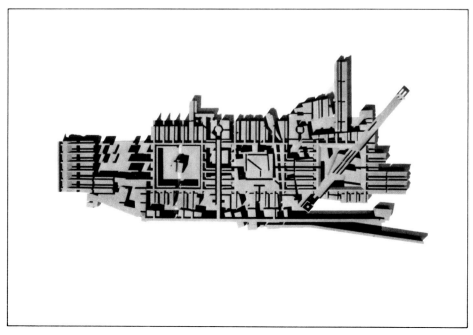

**Feasibility Study for a New College
of Architecture Building,
University of Kentucky**

**Anthony Eardley
With Paul Amatozzo,
Karuthers Coleman, Paul Pinney**

76 This model is the sixth in the development of this feasibility study. This exercise in the formal exploration of a distinct building type is now in its third year, having been conducted intermittently by myself and my colleagues on the College Building Committee at the request of the Vice President for Academic Affairs.

Earlier models in the series were made prior to the assignment of a site on the campus, their purpose being to test in both linear and square configuration plan-forms the programmatic viability of an idea for a building conceived as a *machine à habiter* for architects, and to identify the most basic formal and structural issues involved. These first models were small-scale, color-coded paper studies which examined the distribution of the program areas of the object type within an ideal section comprising: a basement or lower ground-floor level accomodating all the public functions of the school; namely, the combined lecture and exhibition hall, (preferably with access to natural top light, and directly connected to the main entry hall, to a protected outdoor space and to the undergraduate studios on the floor above), the administration and faculty conference suite, a faculty and student *commons* opening to the lecture and exhibition hall open space, and studio space for a future graduate program, and a tall, top lit, attic storey, accomodating the entire undergraduate studios and project review space, with faculty offices and seminar rooms housed in a mezzanine gallery overlooking

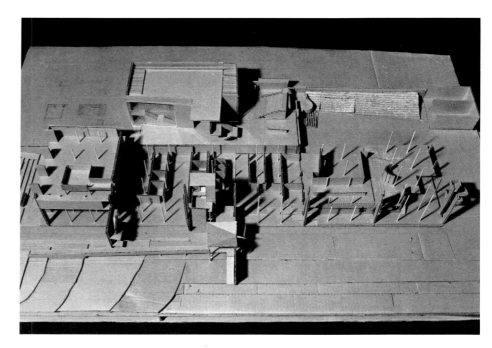

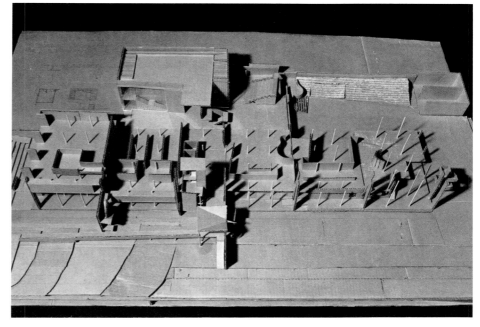

*Feasibility study for a new College of
Architecture Building, University of
Kentucky. Four stages of
cardboard model.*

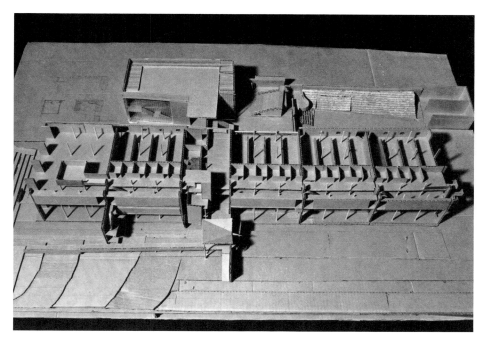

the studio and jury area.

The close coincidences of the program area of this attic storey with that of the basement, and the relatively smaller program area of the intervening public floor permits the workshop at one end of the building and library reading room at the other to become double height spaces representing the two poles of architectural thought and constructive endeavor.

Model number six is built of loosely assembled and easily modified or replaceable elements at one-eighth inch scale. It explores the distortion of the object type in response to the demand of a less than ideal orientation (the city grid is laid out at 45° to north) on a site with few and contradictory contextual elements. The most important development represented in this model, however, is the recognition that the program insists on the establishment of a dialogue between building elements such as the lecture and exhibition hall, which require load-bearing walls, and the main building which was originally conceived as a free plan. The outcome offers the interesting possibility, perhaps first suggested by the Secretariat at Chandigarh, of a fugal composition, but readable in all three dimensions.

House for a Couple of Psychoanalysts

**Diana Agrest and
Mario Gandelsonas**

This "House for a Couple of Psychoanalysts," the last liberal profession to appear in Western culture, should be seen as a late addition to Ledoux' typology of houses for the ideal city. The demand made by the need to accomodate working and living quarters for two psychoanalysts and their children in a party-wall plot is resolved through a sequence of spaces and buildings defining a transition from the public realm to the private world. This transition is established through a dialectic between monumental and domestic contradictory motifs, i.e. arches and porticos versus a pitched roof box; manifested in the sequence of gate/semipublic court, gate/building, private court/house/garden. The gate building which marks the point of transition between public and private realms is an archway with services for the house in the lower level and professional offices in the second level. The house within the sequence is horizontally organized between two transitional figures that define front and back, "reverberating" the previous building in the development of the sequence. In the front, an arch-doorway duplicates the building arch, in the back a double portico expresses the first internal contradiction of the house: public versus private, monumental verses domestic.

The house is organized in terms of a second contradiction—that between fragment and whole—and the architectural implications of this contradiction. The house is vertically structured by the contrast between communal family space (living-dining-kitchen) organized according to an axis perpendicular to the party-walls which defines their presence, and four autonomous double-height "cells" (bedroom-bathroom) with individual access through four spiral staircases which are perceived as four columns in the living area. Each of these four rooms are separated from each other and connected only by a very light passerelle. From the common space below, the rooms are perceived as "floating" individual columns. This organization provides the context for a double *mise-en-scene* of a way of life and a mode of architectural writing. The clients can be seen as a typical family (father, mother, boy, girl), as a hierarchical pyramidal structure. However, the formal organization of the architecture suggests the break of this structure and the possibility of a re-organization where four people live as individuals or as part of a family group related through a variety of associations.

The model of the house condensates and multiplies the representative power of the traditional architectural model and drawing. The traditional architectural drawing fragments the building to produce a knowledge of its parts and relationships. The traditional model verifies the building as an object. In this case the specific qualities of drawing are displaced to the model. This displacement introduces a temporal dimension that fragments the model as object and impregnates it with narrative and sequential qualities.

Models:
Steve Allen
Paul Bodine
Gregory Gall
John Nambu
Jessie Reiser
David Williams
Sarah Wilmer
Leonardo Zylberberg

House for a Couple of
Psychoanalysts, *1978. Model, 1980.*
Mahogany veneer, maple, brass,
metal. Plan and volumetric
relationships.

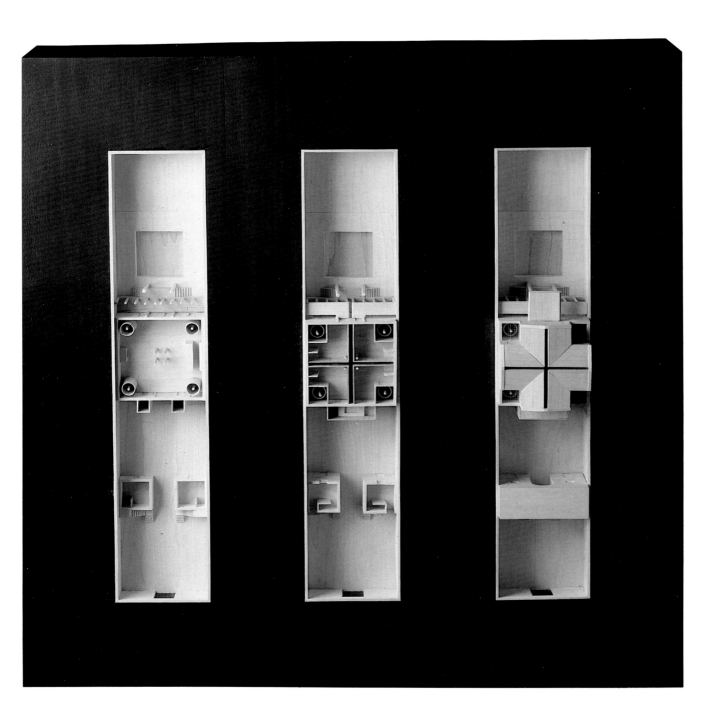

House for a Couple of
Psychoanalysts. *Common space and
private rooms seen from below.*

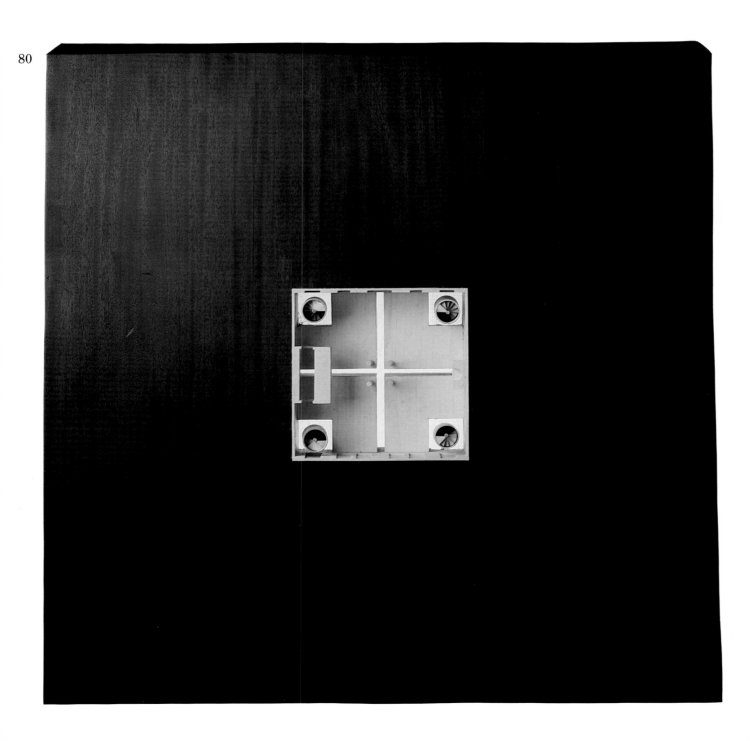

House for a Couple of
Psychoanalysts. *Facades/sections:
sequence through professional, public,
and private spaces.*

House X

Peter Eisenman

The final artifact in the process of making House X is the axonometric model. It was made, if not conceived, after working drawings were finished and after it was decided not to proceed with the actual building of the house. It can thus be seen as the ultimate reality of the work, a final statement of the object's autonomy, and at the same time of the heuristic and approximate nature of the process. Usually a model is stationary and the viewer moves around, above, and even below it to understand its reality; there is no fixed viewpoint. An axonometric drawing, on the other hand, is based on a fixed, usually frontal viewpoint. The information it conveys does not change from different viewpoints. The axonometric *model,* in contrast, changes depending on the position of viewing. From the side and from eye level it is seen as raking in different directions. Then from a slightly raised angle on the oblique it is seen as a conventional orthogonal model. Finally, when viewed from the oblique at a forty-five degree angle with one eye closed, it appears to flatten out and assumes the precise aspect of an axonometric drawing: the viewer, forced into a frontal and monocular view, sees the building as through a camera.

Usually a photograph of a building is a narrative record of a fact—a *representation* of reality. Here the photograph *is* the reality of the model because it is the view which reveals its *conceptual essence* as an axonometric drawing. But while the

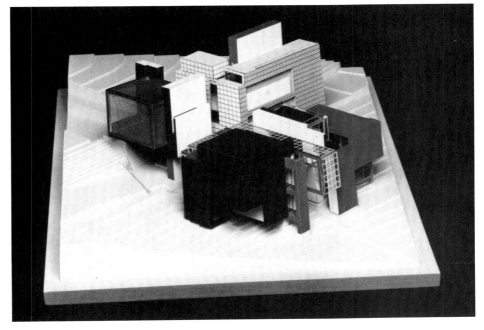

Top left: House X, 1978. Actual axonometric model. Photograph taken to show actual distortion.

Top right: View from northeast photographed to look like an axonometric collage.

Bottom left: Front view photographed to appear as an orthogonal model.

Bottom right: Elevation view of model.

conceptual essence of the model is a drawing, that of the photograph is not. For it is not a photograph of a drawing but of a model...Yet the black and white photograph depicted in this catalogue and the drawing are one and the same. Here the circle is closed, and the true reality of the house remains suspended. The model serves as the final heuristic approximation, the last act of what I call a process of decomposition. The model exists as one reality and simultaneously another.

83

Residence

William Ellis

84 This is a house of vertical planes.
They compress into a hill at one side
to give privacy and protection from
the weather. They gradually unfold
in layers on the other side, opening
toward the sun and a view over a
harbor. They fold over each other to
admit light to the interior. They slip
past each other to form two parts:
a long low wing for guests and work,
and a high layered hall for living and
sleeping.

This house elaborates a variety of
spatial events from an economic
conception.

Residence, 1979. Model.

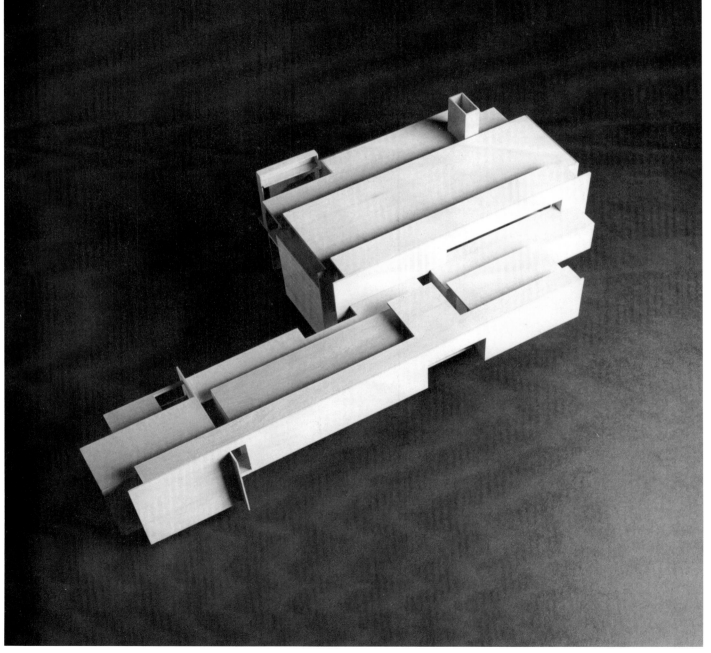

The Sunar Showroom

Michael Graves

Models and drawings serve me primarily as a diary or sketchbook of remembered things, such as a plan or a facade I have thought about or a painting that has particular meaning for me. Similarly, the objects which we collect and with which we surround ourselves have significance in that they not only exist at a material level, but also can serve as models or types which have more general thematic significance. For example, a metronome which has a known utility may also bring to mind, by virtue of its generic form, an obelisk or pyramid. It is thought that the obelisk, in its vertical stance within the landscape, was once an abstract representation of the human figure. Therefore, it is quite possible to see the location of a simple metronome within a painted domestic interior as having significance in an invented interior landscape. The symbolic life of a simple object such as a metronome is potent beyond its pragmatic use.

In a similar manner, the representation of man as Terminus figure has its origins in Roman mythology. In his totemic stance, Terminus stands at the boundary between occupiable space and the profane landscape beyond. He makes, at that boundary line, a frontal confrontation within us as we approach him, but because of his "landscape attire" he can also be seen as part of the larger plane of the forest wall. He is both column and wall, simultaneously represented in one symbolically decorated figure.

Models and drawings are, by nature, tentative inquiries. Seen in series, they document a process of inquiry and examine questions raised by a given intention in a manner which provides a basis for later, more definitive work. In modeling ideas, we are not attempting to make either imitation or real buildings; we are attempting to get at the shared essence that buildings and models both possess. If it is possible to describe, in the best sense of the word, the "aesthetic" of a model, it is that idea which we hope the final work, the building itself, will possess. It is not incumbent on the model to describe the final work, the building, or to be like it in appearances, but it is required for the model to convey its essence or idea. In fact; I think it is impossible to translate directly model into building or drawing into building, as it is impossible to convey directly any thought into a verbal notation, often we even sense that the distortions of an idea conveyed in its corresponding language are not only a positive gesture but, through the process of translation, an area of possible invention. An idea, on the one hand, and its representation, on the other, are similar, of course, and share an essence, but nevertheless they remain separate languages.

Sunar Showroom, 1979. Terminus construction.

"Natural History"

John Hejduk

88   In the 1930s I used to visit the New York Museum of Natural History. I was drawn to the exhibits where animals natural to Africa were shown in three–dimensional panoramas. These scenes were remarkable, for in a very contained and compressed space, great distances in perspective were depicted. I remember always searching for the demarcation line, that is, where the actual three-dimensional object left off and the illusionistic perspective began. I never found that line.

Years later I visited again my favorite spot, but new installations were fabricated. The new scenes were painted and obviously made by new depictors. I was greatly disappointed for I could easily find the demarcation line between the three-dimensional and the two-dimensional. What this meant to me was that the old "realists" had passed on. They had stories to tell.

So I picked a one–inch deep cardboard box, made a crude wood frame around it, and put within the box a small house and a cross-section of a tower. I painted these with watercolors and thought about eighteenth-century Venice.

The Thirteen Towers of Cannaregio,
1979. Model. Paint, wood, cardboard.

Architecture and Building

Massimo Scolari

90 The history of architecture appears as an area of darkness occasionally unveiled in the light of criticism which fits the past into a description and classification of general formulas. Only classical architecture, which the history of criticism and public opinion have endowed with a *second nature* validity, is immune to doubts and hesitations.

All else is inevitably postulated *in spite of* or *because* of it. The reason for this rests perhaps in the fact that architecture is not a science. Unlike the sciences, its rules and precedents are not based on concrete facts which are indisputable in the physical sense. Attributing values or denouncing errors inevitably leads us back to the metaphysical sphere of the "feeling of the times," to the taste of the artists, rather than to objective conclusions. It is ultimately impossible to elaborate scientific formulations that can be discussed rationally.

Science "discovers" the laws of nature, and the sum total of its discoveries forms a theory of facts and truths which are handed down from one generation to the next in an irreversible and hence progressive pattern. The arts, and architecture in particular, on the other hand, appear as a *constant accumulation of possibilities* which the artistic process brings to an equal number of enigmas.

Architecture does not afford an experimental scientific development that might allow the more recent artists to make use of the attainments of their predecessors, thus increasing the chances for further advancement. The "progressions" or steps taken by those who preceded us leave no set course or limitations that constitute a mandatory starting point for those who follow.

The Fall of Icaro. *Mixed media.*

The *Chicago Tribune* Tower

Robert A. M. Stern

92 Our project for the new *Chicago Tribune* Tower takes as its primary reference Adolf Loos's entry in the original 1921-22 competition, and it attempts to marry that project to the Miesian prism. To build a classical tower out of glass, we have used architectural elements rooted in the culture of the past though executed in the technology of the present.

The flat pilaster as opposed to the round column employed by Loos is used in order to retain the shape of the standard office building box. These pilasters are tripled on each face in the manner of Michaelangelo's third story of the Palazzo Farnese, to increase the sense of verticality of the tower, provide multiple corners that add interest to the interior, and increase the opportunities for reflections on the exterior. The corners of the block are quoined in a stripe pattern of black spandrel glass and white frosted glass; this pattern refers to Loos's house for Josephine Baker with its striped articulation, and to the black and white lines of the newspaper itself.

The signboard at the top refers to the cultural conditions of the Midwest which in earlier days gave rise to the urbanism of the false front, and whose nostalgia for the somehow grander things from other places gave rise also to the name *"Chicago Tribune"* with its self-righteous overtones of Roman morality. The Tuscan order of the pilasters best approaches the nostalgia for the presumptive moral austerity and rectitude of the ancient Roman tribunes, while the red and gold color scheme best recalls that period.

The word "Tribune" on the south face of the building is directed to those across the Chicago River in the Loop and announces that in crossing the river one is entering the land where the *Chicago Tribune* pioneered large-scale development. In the same way, recalling Henri Labrouste's "Bridge Connecting France and Italy," the word "Chicago" on the north face announces that one will soon be entering the "real" Chicago of the Loop area—the frame and in-fill architecture of William Le Baron Jenney beloved by Sigfried Giedion—and leaving behind that other Chicago of suburbs and styles, of the cultural complexities of Frank Lloyd Wright, Howard Shaw, and David Adler.

Assistant in charge:
Gavin Macrae-Gibson.

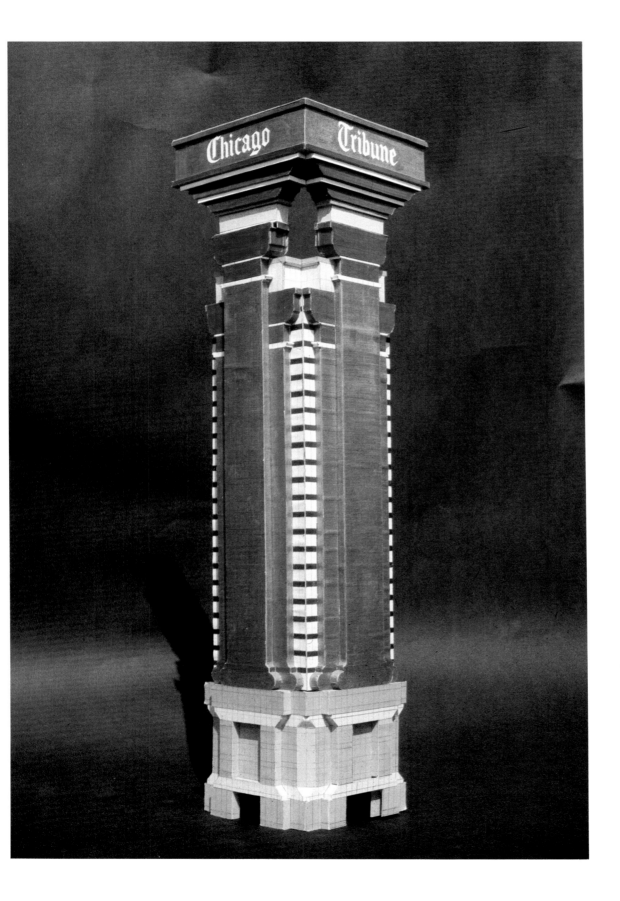

A Doric Round House

Amancio Guedes

Doric Round House. Model. Wood. Two views.

Bottom: Analytical sketches.

94 This round house is the first child of a marriage between a social center I invented sometime ago and a more recent house prototype. Features from both parents are recognizable. It is a little more than half the social center although it bluffs that it is three-quarters. The round-edged terrace is cornered by the two sides of the house as in the previous prototype. The drawing tries to explain some of these connections as well as to demonstrate the adventures of the idea.

The absolute and pure circular walled volume punctured by slits and various-sized round eyes is aimed axially to the north. The rectangular side volume locks the whole to the angle of the street. This forty-five degree angling also enunciates the central entrance to the house, and the center parting of the two curved gables further reinforces this entry.

The circular base splits axially to accomodate an existing change in level on the site.

The house is quite Doric although no Classical details have been superimposed. The model is a layered cake of pine slices.

The orderly balustrades and pergolas which will garland the upstairs terraces have been left out of the model purposely because they would have been too fussy at the reduced scale. They continue an idea of office balconies I invented some nine years ago.

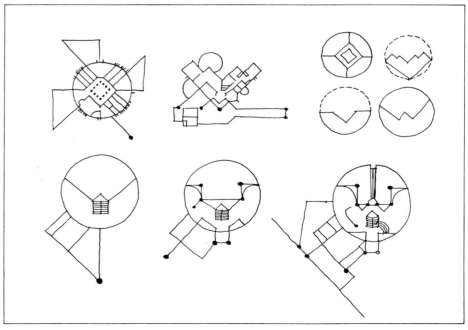

Prototype Housing

Gwathmey Siegel Architects

96   This model is a prototype study for
attached court houses. The prototype—a line of theoretically any
length, repetitive center elements,
and different end conditions—
accomodates multiple variations
within the formal construct. The intention is to maintain a public facade
that is a covered arcade connecting
the separate house entries, and a
private facade that is view-oriented
and volumetrically articulated.

Courthouse prototype. Model.
Mixed media.

Monument

Leon Krier

98 The English telephone box is a masterpiece of English architecture; it has nothing of that unpredictable beast which is kept on the private wall and which has turned the great world into a village tyranny. It is a public object, a monument par excellence; it deserves to be treated and positioned in the city as nothing less.

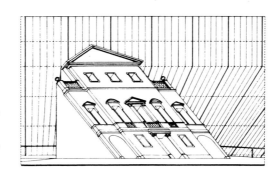

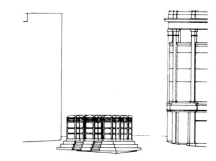

Below: English telephone kiosk monument. Model. Toy models of British standard telephone kiosks, paint, plaster.

Left: Derby Civic Center, 1970. James Stirling, with Leon Krier. Facade of Assembly Hall and telephone kiosk monument.

V-Space

Bernhard Leitner

Right: Model, V-Space. *Mixed media.*

Below: Diagrammatic sketches of sound movement.

100 The V-space is designed for four loudspeakers (1,2,3,4).

A simple line of sound is created by sound moving between a number of speakers. The V-space, however is designed for double lines of sound. Two different frequencies in two spatially separated lousdpeakers determine space. The three illustrations exemplify such stereo spaces in motion.

1. Ascending space: frequency I moves from speaker 2 to speaker 1: simultaneously, frequency II moves from speaker 3 to speaker 4.

2. Double pendulum: the two sound motions swing simultaneously in opposite directions.

3. Ascending, descending, crossing, and swinging spaces move in parallel, expanding, contracting, penetrating each other.

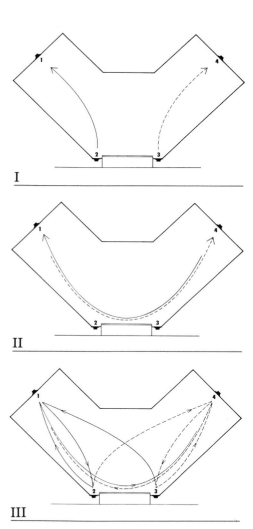

I

II

III

DOM Corporation Headquarters

Rodolfo Machado
Jorge Silvetti

102 This is for us both a model of a project for the headquarters of DOM Corporation and the latest manifestations of a compositional technique of particular interest nowadays inasmuch as it embodies, perhaps, a personal iconographic motif. It involves the *investigation* of an architectural idea in three-dimensional form plus, more importantly, the *demonstration* of its "generative potential" through a specific project.

At the heart of this technique there is a syntactic operation dealing with the notions of superimposition of centers (or architectural elements that have traditionally been regarded as being mutually exclusive), polycentrality (generated by regulated displacement of the centers of parts), and the fragmentation plus interpenetration of types and elements.

Because this technique implies a view of the notion of center that is not classical, maybe even anti-classical, we would like to consider it as of a truly modern architectural nature. We started to develop this technique in our design for the Rhode Island School of Design Freshman Studio ("The Steps of Providence," Machado and Silvetti, 1978-1979), it was continued in a proposal for the *Chicago Tribune* tower ("American Skyscrapers," Machado, 1980), and has recently informed this project.

On Centrality. *Model, Project for DOM Corporation, Cologne, Germany. Plexiglass, cardboard, metallic paint and paper.*

Museum Für Kunsthandwerk, Frankfurt, Germany

Richard Meier

The design for the museum für Kunsthandwerk is a total scheme incorporating a new museum, existing museum buildings, a tree-filled park, and the adjacent embankment along the River Main.

Forming a coherent recreational area for the citizens of the community and city as well as the visitors to the museum, this design forms a pedestrian link between two previously isolated parts of the city, the city center across the river to the north and a major residential area to the south. It invites all to take advantage of the new environment while making a major contribution to the city's urban structure.

Designed to house the arts and crafts treasures now held in the nineteenth-century Villa Metzler, the new museum with its white porcelain-enameled steel facade creates a lightness and elegance of its own, making it the centerpiece of the complex and establishing a unique identity for its collections while complementing the landscape of the park and river embankment. Measuring 209,760 square feet, the new building is an extension of the older Villa Metzler, replicating its dimensions and scale in a basic quadrate form whose axes and grid generate the design of the park as they align with major pedestrian paths, property lines, and existing frontages.

Visitors are guided through a prescribed sequence of exhibits, beginning with an introduction to the museum's masterpieces at a temporary showcase area in the entry hall that entices them to move up the wide ramps into the permanent collection areas on the floors above. Here the architecture guides them through chronologically placed exhibits, enabling them to trace stylistic and formal developments through the ages. Views of the building itself, the park, the Villa Metzler, and the city, offered by bay windows, ramps, and connecting bridges, contrast with the quiet and simple architecture of the collection areas, allowing the displayed objects to create their own environment and offering the visitor a quiet and serene atmosphere for contemplation.

Museum Fur Kunsthandwerk,
Frankfurt, West Germany, 1979.
Cardboard, plexiglass, paint.

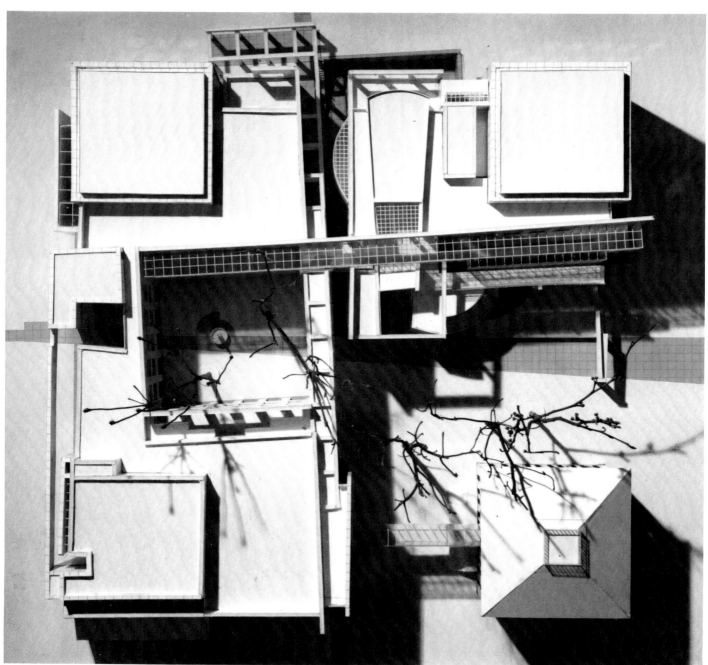

Model-View of a Museum of Roman Art, Mérida, Spain

Rafael Moneo

Museum of Roman Art, Merida, Spain. Relief model. Cardboard.

106 As in my model for the exhibiton, the drawing—a one-point perspective—is materialized by overlaying different planes onto which the dimensions of the drawing have been transferred. Thus, an abstract object is produced without establishing a scalar connection with the projected reality. But the photograph of the model exposes the fiction of reality, giving, in spite of the flatness, a perspectival depth of view.

Bunker Hill Pavilion

Charles Moore

Bunker Hill Pavilion project.
Model fragment. Mixed media.

108   This model, a fragment from a design study, developed out of my participation in an urban design competition for Los Angeles's Bunker Hill. The Bunker Hill project involved four high-rise buildings on a street that is physically and imagistically central to the hill. Between the buildings were carefully scaled courtyards. The pavilion shown in the model was a part of one of the courtyards. It is a simple form with a semi-circular top, and houses a restaurant. The house form is a reproduction of one of the wonderful Victorians that used to exist on Bunker Hill, half in negative and half in positive. The material is reflective glass.

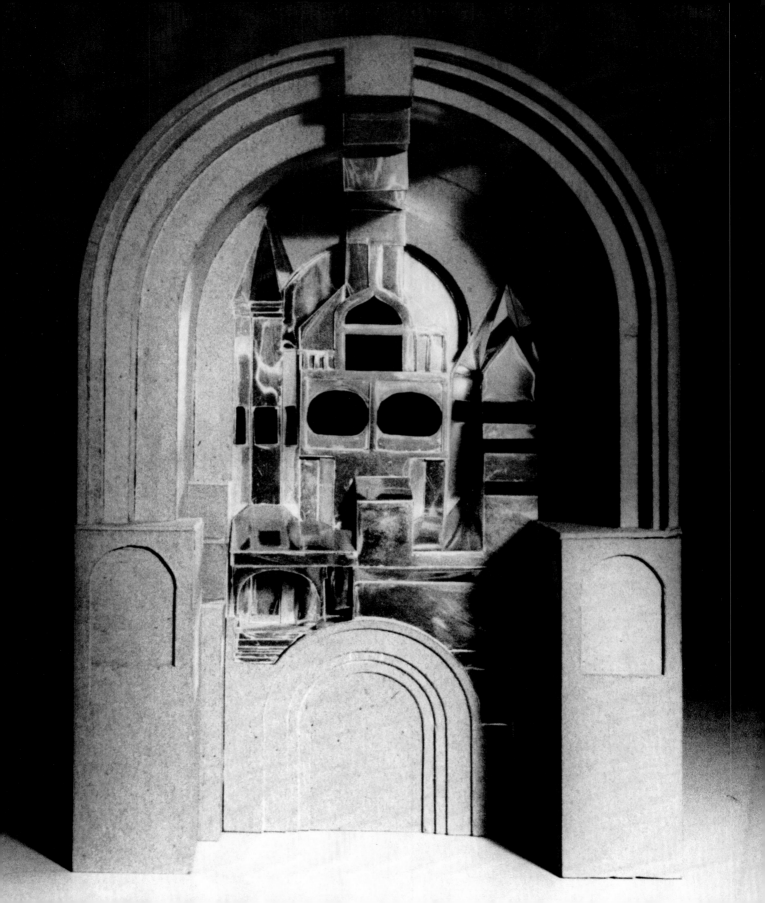

Menges House

Jaquelin Robertson

110 The house, overlooking a tidal pond and the beach in Easthampton, represents a timeless dialogue between external context—both physical and cultural—and internal requirements, and their mediation through the artificial language of architecture.

One intention of the design process was to explore in model form the typology of this hybrid, old/new house, in which a familiar traditional device, the local "twin gable" facade, is employed in the organization of a not-so-traditional program, a contemporary bi-nuclear plan (i.e., children's house/parents' house). By its nature and purpose the exercise recognized and reinforced the residual nature of the "untreated" end elevations: the contents of the book described by its covers.

Two three-dimensional architectural "faces" look in and out, and up and down, suggesting both the inner accommodation and its exterior limits, and focusing the various formal counterpoints: symmetry/asymmetry, front/back, right/left, ground/sky, small scale/large scale; mirror image/distortion, real space/implied space, face/mask. At the same time but in two different voices, these faces make historical quotations and recall the ongoing amendment of the local vernacular by more modern elements and attitudes.

The model is thus both an analytic and a poetic tool which prompts simultaneously semantic and syntactic interpretations, and in a way that is more starkly telling than is the traditional rendering of plan, section, and elevation. It is able to comment and to expand on at least two kinds of meaning and logic in a single reductive format; to suggest a variety of "readings" each logically exclusive yet crucially reinforcing the other.

In this sense the model is the agent of synthesis between form and content, the clearest (and yet the most complex) distillation of the *idea of the house.*

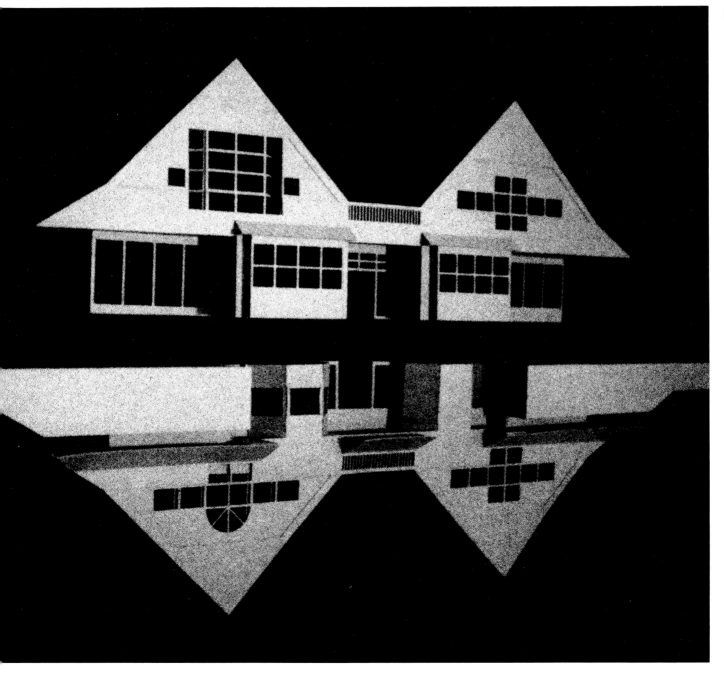

The Little House in the Clouds

Stanley Tigerman

112   This is the story of the primeval house standing under the stars. The house is ordered by sacred pillars with Corinthian capitals supporting a celestial soffit of clouds, suggesting paradise as trompe l'oeil.

We look back once more to the beginning of man in his opposition to nature. Primal man is again viewed in the mirror image of himself, as voyeur trapped in history.

The land inflects as if depressed by the weight of the foreign objects placed upon it. The downward deformation accepts both the house and the trees which are halved with scalpel-like precision. One half of the house returns to nature while the other half becomes man's vestigial home.

Both the house on *pilotis* and its topiary mirror image suggest a ritualistic dance. The earth recedes, removing itself from what might become a struggle or an embrace.

Far into the future as sentinels they stand and they watch and they wait.

House Within a House

O.M. Ungers

114 This model demonstrates the idea of the house within the house or, more generally, the object within the object—the principle of the Russian doll. At the same time, it demonstrates the idea of an indefinite space. To walk from one space to the other is to go from the inside of one space to the inside of the other. There is no outside in this concept. Inside and outside are interchangeable, and therefore the space has no beginning and no end. The fascination of such a conversion of space is meant to create a psychological acceptance of the unmeasurable and unconcealable environment. The result is a dreamlike quality.

More specifically, the model actually consists of four separate house models which are encased within each other. The innermost model represents a stone house; it is a solid block with holes carved out. The second model represents a glass house surrounding the stone house, and it is like a courtyard building. The third model covers both the first and second one with a skeletal structure; it represents a timber post–and–beam house. The fourth model surrounds the previous three and represents a house or space formed by an earth wall and green hedges and trees: it represents an earth house or a nature house.

As one walks through the entire sequence, the material becomes lighter and lighter in weight. From the very solid inner core there is a transformation—in a morphological sense—first into a perforated structure, then into a skeleton or a filigree, and finally into a transparent wall of nature. The architectural concept thus consists of both the morphological transformation of the house from a heavy structure into a transparent filter—which symbolizes a transformation from earth into air—and the idea of the house within the house.

House within a house. *Model. Wood.*

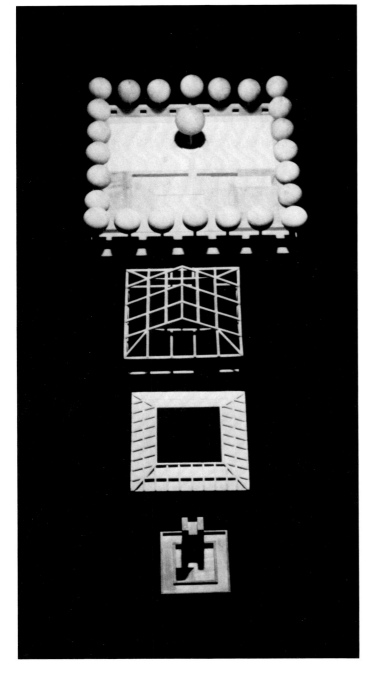

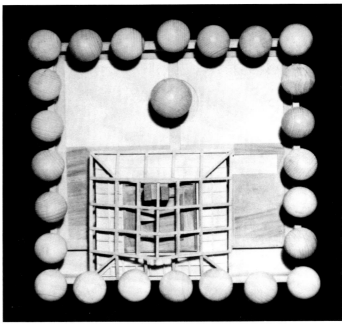

Atrium
235 Fifth Avenue, New York

Tod Williams and Associates,
Architects

116   This 1/4 inch scale model is one of many made for the projected conversion of an airshaft into an atrium. The idea is to lodge a single object at the base of a skylighted shaft. The object gathers each of the activities of the space into its reduced formal presence which reveals a stair, a bridge, a window, a wall, and a fountain.

Both this model and the model in the 1976 exhibition express a concern for the way an object is ultimately realized. Both expect the idea of the building to be capable of being defined in model form. Both use the model to describe an idea about space, and the space about an idea. However, there has been a change in the way I use models. One important change is the introduction of color. Previously the use of white enabled me to describe form before it was altered by color, and to abstract what was a very representational model. Now color is not used literally, but rather as a way of embracing the use of color to describe form while retaining the idea and the object in the realm of the abstract. Previously, models were merely reductions of buildings; now they are objects in and of themselves. Previously the model was used as a representation of an idea which had been very clearly defined before the model was started. Now both the model and the idea develop simultaneously. The models are as precise as before, but more experimental; no longer encased in glass, the potential of the model is greater.

Model: Robert McAnulty, David Warner

Atrium, New York. Model.
Cardboard.

Romeo and Juliette Fountain

Stuart Wrede

118   A reinforced masonry wall of equal
height and width has ivy growing on
both sides of it. On one side a white
marble staircase rises up to a portal
in the wall which leads to a small
balcony also in marble. The balcony
overlooks a semicircular pool of
water out of which rises a dark grey
cylindrical limestone rock,
semispheric at the top, out of which
spouts a jet of water.

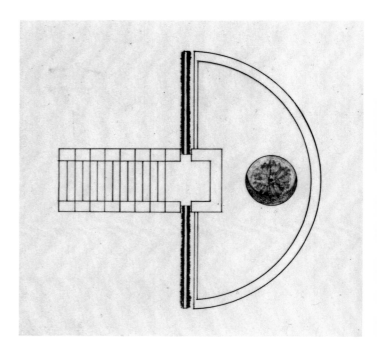

Romeo and Juliette Fountain. *Model.*
Foamcore board, plastic.

Left: Romeo and Juliette Fountain.
Plan and elevation.

Idea as Model 1980

Figure Credits
pp.77-79 Photographs by Dick Frank
p.89 Photograph by Sadin/Karant
p.94 Reprinted from *James Stirling,*
Oxford University Press, 1975.
p.101 Esto Photographics, Inc.,
Wolfgang Hoyt.
p.102,103 Photograph by S. Samso

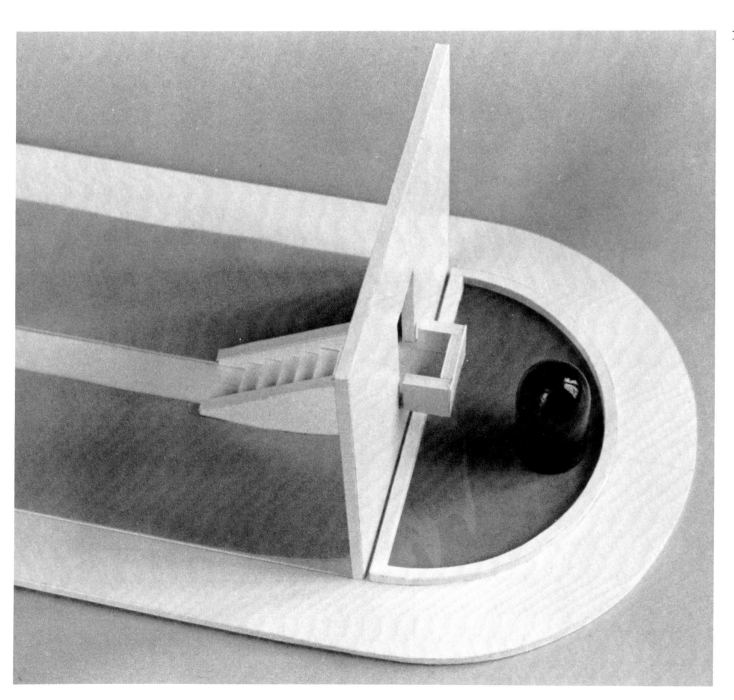

1 *Project for Cannaregio Town Square, 1978. Model.*

A Poetics of the Model: Eisenman's Doubt

Taken from an interview with Peter Eisenman
By David Shapiro and Lindsay Stamm on March 8, 1981

DS: Your architecture might be subtitled "At the sign of the sign." One thinks of *Semiotica's* recent issue on signs about signs. What does this self-reflexivity signify? A model would seem to be the least self-reflexive, the most representational of objects. Since you seem to be wrapped in the drama of self-reflexive palpability, how do you escape the confrontation with the representational model?

PE: What has always been a concern for me is architecture itself, the attempt to separate the notion of the sign from that of the substance. Traditionally, the substance of architecture has been the built building. It was thought to be an object that was symbolic of man or mimetic of his condition. My first concern in looking at the nature of architecture involved an attempt to change the nature of the sign of the substance—from referring to man to referring to architecture itself. This was the first important shift in my work: from the built artifact as the mark of a traditional sign to the building as a sign about itself. My first houses began to question the nature of a sign in architecture, and how a sign is made. The first house was built like a model airplane—the connections between columns and beams were actually sanded down and glued together. House II was built to look like a model (often when the photograph of House II is printed in a magazine, it is mistitled a "model photograph"). Thus, while House I was built like a model, House II actually looked like a model. I was also concerned with the experience of the sign, that is, how does the subject relate to the object? This question suggested that the architectural sign is not like a linguistic sign, since it also has substance and sensuous properties. Fundamentally architecture is involved with sensuous properties, rather than merely with relationships of signs.

DS: It is exactly the sensuousness that may be the linkage with the linguistic system: that is the poetic axis with its musicalist emphasis.

PE: The first two houses questioned the nature of the sign and the capacity of the sign to be self-referential; the next two houses questioned the relationship of this self-referential sign to the substance and the poetics of the sign; and finally the last two houses posed the problem of representation in terms of the idea of scale, which ultimately led to the idea of the model. The exhibition "Idea as Model" was initiated in order to find out if other architects also dealt with these problems of representation and scale.

In figurative sculpture the size of the maquette is usually known, since it represents some known object. Modern sculpture shifted from representation to abstraction and thus from scale-specific to scale non-specific—that is, it became self-referential. How large is a Brancusi or a Sol LeWitt? When sculpture ceased to be anthropomorphic, it became scale non-specific. Since architecture, on the other hand, was always scale-specific, an architectural model could always be related to at its own level, as it was evidently smaller that the scale of human use.

LS: But doesn't scale specificity vanish in the case of the contemporary superblock or megastructure?

PE: Mario Gandelsonas has made the point in the case of Aldo Rossi's Gallaratese that the whole issue of scale is very clear: the scale of the city on the outside, the scale of the individual and the living cell on the inside, and the disassociation between the two. The window in the Gallaratese is too large for the interior room, but it is the right scale for the city. For me, this disassociation of the exterior and interior scale is self-referential. What makes Rossi's architecture interesting is that rather than referring to the individual scale it refers to this displacement between interiority and exteriority.

DS: It is difficult to discuss scale without mentioning the sublimity of Romanticism, which served in part to break down, to terrify by inhuman or antihuman scale. I was wondering if your escape from scale could be construed as a kind of romanticism.

PE: My concern with the architectural model could be understood in two ways. One would be as a representation of ideas (as opposed to of buildings). For example, Rossi's drawings are not about an architecture to be built; they are not even drawings of architecture. They are drawings of architectural ideas. The second would be the model as an idea

2 *House El Even Odd, 1980. Model.*
View from above.

3 *House 11a, 1978. Model.*

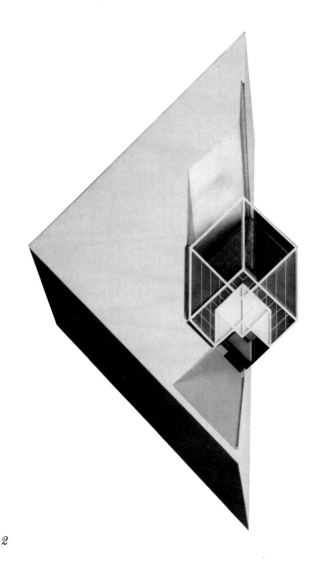

2

in itself, an object as was the case with the House X model. It is not a representation of anything. I suppose in both cases I would use the term hermeticism rather than romanticism.

LS: Did your exploration of the notion of the self-referential model start with House X or were models crucial to the conception of your work prior to House X?

PE: Prior to House X, models were used as notational references, as in the case of the House II model where the elements were color-coded. In fact, as it turned out, the *only* way you could understand the structure of House II was through the model, since you could not experience the notations explicitly in the built object itself.

LS: Did the models reveal the structure in a manner that was not possible in the series of diagrammatic drawings?

PE: In the case of House II the model was made out of plexiglass, because when certain forms overlay each other in a drawing they became confusing. Only the model allowed the elements to come apart and be seen. A drawing always has a fixed point of view, while you can walk around a model. This was the motivation behind the development of the axonometric model in House X. It was based on the supposition that the model could not be appropriated in a conventional way if it was regarded as the reality. However, in this case, the reality of the model could only be seen from a fixed viewpoint and not from the actual, three-dimensional experience. When you apporached the tilted model and moved around it, the model seemed like a distortion. Any displacement from the fixed viewpoint at once revealed the falsity of the model. This particular model was not about the house at all; it was about the nature of another kind of object and another kind of reality. In other words, in the model of House X the monocular view at 45° is the only way of seeing the reality which the model possesses. The model forces you into this view, which only a camera can achieve, and with the photograph (in this case, the ultimate reality) it is transformed from a model into a two-dimensional representation.

LS: Is that not diametrically opposed to the notion of

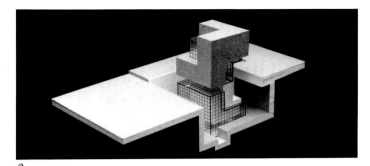

3

decomposition that is inherent in this particular project?

PE: Of course, it has nothing to do with the idea of decomposition. The axonometric model came after the idea of decomposition. It does not even necessarily have to be about House X. However, it did serve as a conclusion to a project that was not going to be built—as a final distancing of subject and object.

LS: Does that axonometric model have a condensed sense of actual and virtual space?

PE: The issue of virtual and actual space is not a primary reference in House X. I realized as I was working on House X that a model could be about something other than a representation of reality; it could be reality itself, and at the same time it could be a distortion of that reality. Its physical presence was to have nothing to do with the idea of its presence. An axonometric model fixes the viewpoint of the viewer. Simply because of its smaller scale with respect to the individual who walks around it, it challenges the traditional idea of possessing the model as an object. In an axonometric model, no possession is possible, except from a particular viewpoint. You then understand that the model is no longer a model, for it has, in a sense, become a drawing. The axonometric model investigates the nature of the model, the nature of scale, and the relationship of these factors to the individual, who can no longer possess it. The viewer is forcibly distanced from it. There are three variations on this idea: House X, the project for Cannaregio, and House El Even Odd.

The project for Cannaregio took House 11a and built it as three differently scaled objects. One of the objects is about four feet high; it sits in the square and is the model of a house. You can look at it and think "well, that is not a house; it is the model of House 11a." Then you take the same object and put it in House 11a; you build House 11a at human scale—and you put this same model of it inside. The object which occupies the main space now is this four-foot-high model of House 11a, which sits inside what seems to be another, real-life House 11a.

LS: Is this model inverted as a miniaturization inside House 11a?

PE: When you put the model of House 11a inside, it is no longer a model, becuase once you monumentalize it, it becomes the object itself. By putting the model or smaller object inside the larger object, the larger object memorializes the smaller one. Once the object inside is memorialized, it is no longer the model of an object; it has been transformed from the original four-foot-high object which was a model of something into a real thing. As a consequence, the larger house, the one at anthropomorphic scale, no longer functions as a house.

Then there is a third object, which is larger than the other two, larger than "reality," larger than an anthropomorphic necessity. This completes the reflexive cycle, because the largest one contains both the middle-sized one and the little one. It becomes a musuem of all these things. Because of the change in scale, all three take on different names and different meanings, not in relationship to the individual but to their own change in scale—they become reflexive. Because of the changes in scale, these objects suggest a whole series of other ideas which have nothing to do with the size of man in relationship to the size of the object (whether it is bigger than man, the right size, or smaller). This three-stage process led me to House El Even Odd, where one begins with what appears to be an axonometric model but which itself becomes the reality. Then this reality in turn is transformed: it becomes an axonometric drawing and simultaneously a plan of itself. The supposed model of House El Even Odd is not the model at all; again, it has become another reality.

DS: Linguistically, this would be comparable to the parenthesis becoming the poem. In Raymond Roussel, the parenthesis takes over so that it is as if the larger parts of the sentence have become distinguished from, or subordinated to, the parenthesis.

PE: What happens in House El Even Odd is that when you make a plan of it, it looks like an axonometric; and when you project it as an axonometric, it looks like a plan. So there is a complete reversal, and a curious dislocation occurs that has nothing to do with the object itself. These ideas only become apparent because a plan is not a reality, but merely a projection of reality. House El Even Odd, as it was on the wall in the Castelli Gallery, became yet another reality. And ultimately it is really a hermetic object since it does not require a change in scale; it does not involve the idea of a model.

LS: It does have a preferred reading, though, as it is hung in a planar, frontal fashion on the wall.

DS: What if it was accused not so much of hermeticism, but of a kind of modern mannerism? Manfredo Tafuri and Christopher Lasch have challenged this kind of speculation as a form of narcissism, as a kind of blurring which smirks at reality. What would be your defense?

PE: If one looks at Palladio's architecture, it can be seen as a rereading of the notion of perspective put forward by Brunelleschi and Bramante. Perspective, a mode of representation, changed the relationship of the viewer to the object, and the way the viewer moved in relation to the object became very important. Palladio changed that relationship by using perspective as a mode of representation appropriate to a new distanced subject. He forced the object to have distance from the subject within the framework of the perspective by flattening out the object, by distorting the actual perspective, by making it be more like a drawing, more representational. Today in a world which is no longer anthropocentric, relationships are in some way less hierarchical in terms of subject and object. One of the ways of confronting this more relativistic condition might be through the use of the axonometric mode of representation. If the axonometric is used as the standard means of representing an object, a means which has nothing to do with the way man views it, it is then neither romantic nor in fact hermetic. It begins to open up the limits of the discipline of architecture to further study, as Palladio did.

DS: Do you look at an axonometric the way Jasper Johns looked at a given—that is to say, do you receive it as a cliché?

PE: What the axonometric model does is both distort and open up an investigation into representation. It is no longer *just* a means of representation! It becomes an idea in itself, and an idea about objects, rather than just a manner by which objects may be distanced from the subject.

LS: You talked about the lack of scale specificity in modernist sculpture. How do you define the difference between sculpture and architecture?

PE: Architecture has traditionally been scale-specific. The Cannaregio project attempted an architecture (as opposed to sculpture) which was scale non-specific.

LS: Well, doesn't that tie it to modernist sculpture?

PE: It does, in one sense, but it was attempting to discover what is the limit, to move toward the point where architecture becomes sculpture. One of the limits is obviously the notion of scale. When something is no longer scale-specific, it supposedly becomes sculpture. It asks: is it *possible* to make a scale non-specific architecture, one which still is limited by basic notions which define "architecture," such as shelter, use, construction?

DS: You have said that the three signs of the model—the axes of the model—are scale, time, and representation. Kenneth Frampton has recently said that a model rarely yields the "true experience" of the building. You have cast a razor blade of doubt over what any true experience might be. What is your sense of the experience of building as opposed to a model?

PE: Let us talk about the question of experience in terms of time. Time used to be cumulative for me, as in my first houses. The first diagrams yielded, as in chess, a series of other moves, which eventually led to a conclusion or a product. By House VI, this had changed. House VI is a sequence of diagrams which are nonsequential, which merely describe sign and substance. The house object, the physical substance of the house, is like a film—a series of stills that run together. To understand the house you have to reverse the process and take it apart. You have to return it to a series of still images. The only way to understand the house is to go backward in time.

LS: Is this something that is done conceptually or can it be done literally while one is in the house?

PE: You cannot understand the house when you are literally in it, but you do realize that the house is the result of some process.

DS: What is the relationship of your drawing to your modelmaking? Can you pose equally radical questions in the case of drawing, or have you used the idea of sculpture rather than drawing in your architecture?

PE: Aldo Rossi draws architecture, and his built architecture is often less than his drawn architecture.

LS: Do you feel that statement is also valid concerning the relationship of your drawings to your built architecture?

PE: No, because I do not draw the same way that Rossi does.

LS: Can your comment on Rossi's "drawn architecture" be extended to your models?

PE: I would say that it is true of my modelmaking.

DS: Rossi's drawings are full of the same doubt as that which you place in your models.

PE: My drawings are merely cartoons for the models. The model becomes the focal point—not the drawing.

DS: Roman Jakobson talks about the addresser and the addressee. You have not been able to delete the expressive modes completely. Who is the "you" in your models, since you talk about an end to anthropocentric scale? What is the Modulor of Peter Eisenman, in this sense? Tafuri regards your written texts as analogous to the snare of your buildings—cages, staircases to nowhere, trap rooms which are blocked off. What is your sense of the subject? Michel

Foucault speaks of the death of man as much as the death of God. Are you proclaiming the death of the "you," the end of the audience?

PE: The "you" for me becomes a more relative "you." It is not an anthopocentric "you" or the "you" that relates to theocentricism or technocentricism. It refers to no hierarchy. These blockages that you talk about are attempts to avoid (or relativize) the formerly hierarchical relationships of the "you" to the object, to nature, and to technology. Once the notion of hierarchy is put aside, other phenomena will appear in the relationship of the object to the individual.

DS: You are often associated with rule systems and generativity, and you are asking what the rules are for making the poetic. Jakobson says the rule making the poetic actually is known in the relationship of grammar and geometry. I identify you with this dark rule system, and the wise passivity it implies.

You are a man who is more comfortable with the wise acceptance of the given, an axonometric that you did not create. Jasper Johns said (to paraphrase): I did not design the American flag, that's why I like it. Yours is a finding: *ars inveniendi*.

PE: That is right, because I am not an inventor. I have no capacity to invent. In fact, why I do architecture as opposed to painting is that much of the structure is preordained, whereas in painting, where do you begin, what do you do, what would I paint? I never have to worry about that in architecture. In architecture the limits of what I am interested in are so clearly unresolved and unexplored that there is almost too much to do without worrying about invention.

DS: And so you seem to have shifted from a program for the subject to a disclosure that the subject is in doubt. Your model, like that of Cézanne and Johns, *is* doubt.

Figure Credits
Photographs by Dick Frank

IAUS Exhibition Catalogues

Series 1

126   *Catalogue 1*
Massimo Scolari: Architecture
Between Memory and Hope
Introduction by Manfredo Tafuri

Catalogue 2
Aldo Rossi in America: 1976 to 1979
Introduction by Peter Eisenman

Catalogue 3
Idea as Model
Introduction by Richard Pommer

Catalogue 4
The Princeton Beaux-Arts:
From Labatut to the Program of Geddes
Introduction by Anthony Vidler

Catalogue 5
Robert Krier: Projects About Urban Space
Introduction by Andrew MacNair

Catalogue 6
The Architecture of O.M. Ungers
Introduction by Rem Koolhaas

Catalogue 7
Five Houses: Gwathmey/Siegel Architects
Introduction by Kenneth Frampton
Preface by Ulrich Franzen

Catalogue 8
Ivan Leonidov: Russian Constructivist, 1902-1959
Introduction by Gerrit Oorthuys

Catalogue 9
Philip Johnson: Processes
Preface by Craig Owens
Introduction by Giorgio Ciucci

Catalogue 10
A New Wave of Japanese Architecture
Introduction by Kenneth Frampton

IAUS Exhibition Catalogues

Series 2

Catalogue 11
Wallace Harrison: Fifty Years of Architecture
Introduction by Rem Koolhaas

Catalogue 12
John Hejduk: 7 Houses
Introduction by Peter Eisenman

Catalogue 13
Austrian New Wave
Introduction by Friedrich Achleitner
Essay by Rudolf Kohoutek